An Introduction
to Family Therapy

An Introduction to Family Therapy

VINCENT D. FOLEY, Ph.D.

GRUNE & STRATTON

A subsidiary of Harcourt Brace Jovanovich, Publishers

New York   San Francisco   London

Library of Congress Cataloging in Publication Data

Foley, Vincent D
    An introduction to family therapy.
    Bibliography: p.
    1. Family psychotherapy. I. Title.
DNLM: 1. Family therapy. WM430 F663i
RC488.5.F64   616.8'915   74-11374
ISBN 0-8089-0846-4

Grune & Stratton, Inc.
111 Fifth Avenue
New York, New York 10003

Distributed in the United Kingdom by
Academic Press, Inc. (London) Ltd.
24/28 Oval Road, London NW 1

Library of Congress Catalog Card Number 74-11374
International Standard Book Number 0-8089-0846-4
Printed in the United States of America

To Ann—the growing edge of my life.

Contents

Acknowledgments

This book has grown out of a number of experiences over the past several years attempting to communicate the field of family therapy to university students. In one way or another it owes thanks to a number of people.

To the Most Rev. Francis J. Mugavero, Bishop of Brooklyn, for his support and interest; to the Rev. Joseph M. Sullivan, director of Catholic Charities in Brooklyn; to the Rev. George T. Deas whose friendship and wisdom has been cherished for over 20 years; to the Dr. White Community Center, especially its director Sr. Francis Mary, for the opportunity to put family theory into practice—all are thanked.

To Dr. E. Mark Stern of Iona College for his encouragement in pursuing further study in the field of therapy; to Dr. Kenneth Mitchell of the Menninger Foundation who introduced us to family therapy; to Richard Bollinger, also of the Menninger Foundation, who supervised initial efforts in the field with kindness and tact; to Dr. Homer Jernigan and Dr. Merle Jordan of Boston University for their time and insight into family therapy; to Dr. Marvin Snider of Danvers, Massachusetts, for an insightful critique of an early draft of this material; to Dr. Thomas Fogarty and Dr. Philip Guerin of Albert Einstein College of Medicine for illuminating discussions of Murray Bowen; to Dr. Paul Franklin of the Family Institute for his supervision; to Virginia Satir for a personal communication; to Jay Haley for a private interview; to the late Nathan Ackerman for two long interviews—all are gratefully acknowledged.

ix

To Donald A. Bloch, director of the Nathan W. Ackerman Family Institute, for his encouragement in the writing of the text; to Dr. John Pearce of Cambridge, Massachusetts, who has served a myriad of roles as encourager, criticizer, editor, and friend; finally, to Mrs. Mary Sydor of St. John's University for typing and correcting the manuscript; a special thank you is due.

Foreword

The education of a psychotherapist consists fundamentally in learning about other people's lives, particularly in the contexts of their families, communities, and jobs. There are many difficulties in acquiring this knowledge. First of all, we know a good deal about ourselves and our own families, but as we look at others we are mostly predisposed to see the ways in which they are like us and not to really see the differences. When we do see the differences we at first tend to feel an overwhelming sense of the family's complexity. Indeed individual psychotherapists complain of just that when they begin to see families. As we gradually understand, the impression of complexity fades and we see the individual or family as a unique system composed of reasonable straightforward elements of enormous variability. The uniqueness is a result of the blend of these elements. Among these elements are individual temperament as determined by biological endowment, unique family cultures as shaped by historical chance such as paranoia and death fears rooted in murder or genocide in a previous generation, widely shared ethnic traits such as the ambivalence and guilt that many Irishmen feel toward their intrusively self-sacrificing women, family constellations such as the domineering overprotectiveness of the oldest sibling in many large families, and the impact of social settings such as the frequent moves to new cities and neighborhoods that complicate the lives of military and corporate executive families. There is a tremendous amount to be learned about all these elements.

   In addition to learning so much there are built-in difficulties that stem from the fact that the therapist is the same kind of creature as that which he studies. Like his patients his vision is limited by his ecological niche. In any training institution or private practice he deals with some particular slice of life. His choice of explanatory concepts, diagnostic labels, and treatment strategies evolves to fit that context. Sometimes mismatches do occur when therapists treat people they do not understand.

Like patients, therapists best understand life stages that they have passed through. For example at a Veterans Administration hospital many young men are admitted when upset about the birth of new baby in their family. Childless young therapists find it hard to understand why. Older therapists with children do not.

Probably the most fundamental limitation that we face is the fact that our lives are as short (or long) as those of the people we want to understand. It takes some five to ten years to see what is going to happen in someone's life. How are we to learn from our experience? With time we change and can hardly remember what it was that we did as therapists in our earlier years. We usually think we would do differently today. No doubt we will do our work still differently in future years. And all the while our culture changes around us— changing us all.

Another limitation stemming from the context in which practice is conducted which is not widely discussed is the critical impact of treatment methods on theory. When patients are seen alone and the therapist does not have first hand knowledge of the family, then intra-psychic theories seem to be the only way to make sense of the (often very hard to understand) person. In time the individual therapist and patient establish an alliance and form a mini-family (the transference) in which many of the phenomena of the original family can be observed and dealt with. But it is all conceptualized only in terms of events within the patient's head and neglects the impact of current life in fixing the patient in his problems. Furthermore, making a virtue of the limitation, some therapists believe that it is only in the transference that cures are achieved and that all important issues come up in the transference. By its nature the transference is skewed toward what is possible in that dyadic context, i.e. repeating of dyadic patterns, particularly parent-child, and triads consisting of a dyad and an imagined third person. Also fantasy is emphasized. That is a great deal, but not everything. People have problems stemming from sibling relationships, conflict free but generally maladaptive family patterns, and, most commonly of all, frozen extended family systems. Work from the transference perspective tends to miss these.

Group therapy (i.e. groups of strangers) is limited by the competition for group time and opportunity for leisurely reflection. The strength of groups is their tremendous capacity to induce conformity to group norms, encourage action, and directly provide people with new experiences. Both Transactional Analysis and Gestalt Therapy theory are strongly flavored by their origins in group therapy with an emphasis on rapid decisions and action.

The limitations of the family point of view seem to be less a matter of theory and more practical. A therapist can not expect to learn everything he needs to know by seeing the family as a whole. He may need to know his patient in a number of contexts, particularly the one to one. Also, even when family interviews allow the therapist to see what he must deal with the capacity of a family system to resist change can be tremendous. The therapist may do well to shift his approach to individual or group methods.

It may throw some light on the fragmentation of the psychotherapy profession to point out that some of the above limitations are institutionalized. Similar therapists with similar ideas get together, increasingly agree that they do not think much of some other people's ideas, and set up a self perpetuating organization. As they get older their interests turn elsewhere and change is out of the question. For example in New Haven, Connecticut in the 1960's individual therapists often said that they should like to try group techniques. They didn't and it was only the influx of therapists trained in group work that brought group therapy to town. Indeed, it appears that change occurs almost entirely by generational succession in the context of changing culture.

Obviously the education of a psychotherapist is a life time job. Where do we begin? The answer is largely personal. I have proceeded and still do proceed mostly along the lines that Dr. Foley has followed in this book: combining many concepts and something of the personal approach of the pioneers. I have collected all the ideas that I can find that might be relevent to the work. The mind is limited; I can only use a few concepts at a time. I need a well stocked collection from which I may be able (pre-logically) to pick out the several concepts that are pertinent to a particular family problem. I have learned to imitate innovative therapists in order to look at families through (my version) of their eyes and see something that I would not have seen. Nathan Ackerman, Murray Bowen, Don Bloch, Sal Minuchin, and Joe Chassell (my own therapist) have been my models. By getting to know them, watching live demonstrations, movies and videotapes; reading books and papers; and teaching their ideas to others,—in time something of their perspective is a part of me.

To be a person is to be imbedded in a context and to have one's vision limited and augmented by that context, which of course changes with time. Our scientific tradition leads us to long for the position of the angel in which everything can be seen clearly and finally. But we find that in principle that certainty is denied us. What we can do is to learn all the ideas we can and to share the vision of innovators.

John K. Pearce, M.D.
Cambridge, Massachusetts

Introduction

THE SCOPE OF THIS STUDY

In the past 10 years the number of courses offered in universities bearing the title "family counseling" or "family therapy" has proliferated. Unfortunately this increase has produced many problems for the student, who signs up for a course in the "family." Frequently, the student is given a list of assigned writers and told to read their works and submit reports on what he has learned. With very few exceptions the books and periodicals are extremely difficult to locate even in well-stocked libraries. Even after finding what he needs, the student faces another problem, namely, the differences between authors. Some students are unable to evaluate what they read because they are unable to put the material into some kind of perspective. They need a structure which will give them an approach to the field of family therapy to enable them to understand and to evaluate the material in perspective.

Until now no such instrument existed in the field of family therapy. A psychology student, for example, can find any number of guides or outlines which will give him an idea of his field and some basic understanding of what the similarities and differences are between behaviorism and existentialism. He can read B. F. Skinner or Rollo May within a context and in relation to other theorists of human behavior. The student of family therapy, however, cannot find such a guide or outline.

1

The purpose of *An Introduction to Family Therapy* is to give the student a framework within which he can understand what he is studying—what has happened and what is happening in the field of family therapy. This textbook is meant for the university student who is probably taking a one-semester course, perhaps, at best, 14 or 15 sessions during the year. Just as a teacher faces the limitation of time so also an author faces a limitation of space. This necessarily means that many ideas, some of which are most complex, must be telescoped into a few pages. This results in some of the richness of thought being lost or at least diminished, and also that some thinkers are omitted or given less space than others. However, within that limitation of time, the student, guided by his teacher, should get a firm grasp on the major ideas in the field.

An Introduction to Family Therapy is basically a primer because it is meant to be an introduction to the field of family therapy. Reading a certain theorist becomes more understandable when the student knows beforehand what the theorist's major insights are and how he relates to other thinkers. Whatever reduces the anxiety level of students when faced with a new area of learning should be of great value.

Although this book can be read apart from a course context by an interested reader, nevertheless, it is basically intended to be a tool for the student which is enhanced greatly by the presence of a knowledgeable teacher. *An Introduction to Family Therapy* provides a guideline through the maze of a complex field. It is an instrument which will make teaching a course in family therapy easier for the instructor.

This book is concerned with ideas rather than techniques. It does not focus on how one might go about doing family therapy, nor is it a how-to-do-it guidebook. It is aimed at students more than practitioners, although it does not exclude them. The only way one can develop into a skilled family therapist is by constant contact in the field under the supervision of professionals. The skill cannot be learned out of a book, however sophisticated, and especially from a book aimed at beginners. With this *caveat* in mind, we can begin our introduction to the field of family therapy.

WHAT IS FAMILY THERAPY?

Perhaps the basic issue of family therapy was best stated by the late Nathan Ackerman, not long before his untimely death:

The most striking feature of our field today is the emergence of a bewildering array of diverse forms of family treatment. Each therapist seems to be doing "his own thing." We are faced squarely with the challenge to evaluate this diversity. Which of the differences are real? Which more apparent than real? Does the dramatic quality of these differences, in effect, obscure the basic sameness?(1)

Following Ackerman's suggestion, we will try to sift through the abundant material in the field with the aim of evaluating the diversity. Is it possible to see real differences in approach? Are there common-alities under which all therapists operate? Finally, and most basically, what do we mean by family therapy, how do we define the term? Does it involve the number of people seen together? Or is it more an attitude or approach rather than a question of counting heads?

Given that some family therapists see only couples, and others see multiple families, and still others see an entire social network, it is imperative that we at least have some working definition of family therapy. In an excellent review of marital and family therapy, David Olson suggests that any intervention focusing on the family system rather than the persons in it merits the name of *family therapy*. (2)

Family therapy is centered on the family system and the changes that can be made in that system. The patient, one might say, is the family and its interaction and the individual member is more a symptom of a sick system. This way of thinking is revolutionary for many people and its practical consequences are great.

We see then that in family therapy a new *gestalt* is formed with the family in the foreground and the individual member in the background reversing the more traditional way of seeing the individual person as sick and of prime concern and the family only as background. This new picture leads to new ways of doing therapy.

Within this definition of family therapy there are four distinguish-able approaches: conjoint family therapy, multiple impact therapy, network therapy, and multiple family therapy. The differences in these approaches are mainly in the realm of practice rather than theory and do not constitute different schools of family therapy. All accept the basic notion that the locus of pathology is not the individual person but the system although the concept of system may mean the nuclear family for some and a much wider social network for others.

Conjoint family therapy refers to that situation in which a therapist meets with a family and attempts to focus on the patterns of interaction in the family. It often means that the whole family is present but this is not absolutely required as long as the focus is on family pathology and not just on the pathology of this or that member. Some call this approach to therapy *conjoint psychtherapy.*(3) Murray Bowen calls it *family group therapy.*(4) Whatever name one gives it, the distinguishing mark is a focus on the family.

Multiple impact therapy refers to an approach in which several members of a team work with individual members and various familial combinations for an intensive period of 2 or 3 days.(5) Some feel that the family is overwhelmed by the onslaught of therapists and that by a constant bombardment of family defenses, real change is made possible. Here again, the focus is on the family system.

Network therapy expands therapy from the nuclear family to concerned others, including neighbors, friends, and significant others, and this is considered necessary or helpful.(6) The aim of network therapy is "retribalization," that is, creating a viable social network for the person or family in distress. Based primarily on the thinking of R. D. Laing, the basic notion of network therapy is that such "tribes" or social networks have within themselves the power to heal. Furthermore, this power is attributed to mental illness being the result of a breakdown in traditional social networks which historically have given people a sense of belonging and coping. Illness is the result of alienation not only of a person from a sense of self but from his roots. Therapy then is the attempt to "retribalize" such a person. Again, it is a question of the person being evaluated not in isolation but within a context of a wider social pattern.

Multiple family therapy refers to an approach in which a number of families are seen at the same time. This method, first used by Peter Laqueur, is gaining in popularity.(7,8) The use of other families tends to overcome some of the distance between the therapist and his clients. The author has experienced this when dealing with black, disadvantaged families. The opportunities for observing, imitating, and identifying with other families is increased, and this seems to mitigate some of the barriers between therapist and family. A basic premise, however, is the use of a system approach to therapy.

As noted, family therapy focuses not on the kind of intervention made but on the locus of pathology. Any approach, therefore, in which the therapist sees pathology as residing in the system or interaction can be called family therapy. This is true even if at a given session only the marital dyad is seen or quite possibly only one member of the family. It is not the number of members present that constitutes family therapy but the conception of the therapist.

A BRIEF HISTORY OF FAMILY THERAPY

The roots of family therapy can be traced back to one of Freud's most famous cases. In 1909, Freud treated a young client "Hans" by dealing with him through his father.(9) Nevertheless, despite the importance of this case, Freud decided not to see the families of patients but to work with the person and his problems apart from the family context. The person was the client and the family was only the background. In later times psychoanalysts were quite insistent on separating the client and family as they felt this muddied the transference process which was crucial in treatment.

In the social sciences there were also investigators who were examining cultural influences on personality. In particular, anthropology made a valuable contribution to an increased knowledge of the importance of the family in the formation of personality.(10)

In psychiatry, the work of Harry Stack Sullivan is significant.(11) Sullivan stressed the role of the interpersonal in the development of personality. His insight into the mother-child relationship led to his placing the locus of pathology in the interaction of the two.[11(pp 110-135)] This was a major step in therapy as it moved from seeing the person as patient to taking into account the interpersonal as a critical part of pathology.

One must also mention the thinking of Alfred Adler who stressed the importance of social urges in the development of personality.(12) Adler saw man not as an isolated person but as a social being who moves toward others. Today, some family counselors base their approach to family on Adler's concepts.(13)

However, although family therapy, as we know it today, has its roots in Freud, Sullivan, Adler, and the social sciences, it got its basic impetus from a series of relatively unrelated observations made in the decade 1950–1960.

In 1951, Ruesch and Bateson wrote a book on the role of feedback and information theory in communication.(14) In 1956, the late Don Jackson together with Gregory Bateson, Jay Haley, and John Weakland, using communication theory, developed the notion of the double bind which was to become a central concept among family theorists.(15)

In 1957, Christian Midelfort, working at Lutheran Hospital in La Crosse, Wisconsin, published his findings. After treating the relationship of client and family to schizophrenia, depression, paranoid illness, and neurosis, Midelfort concludes: "This study substantiates the idea that all mental illness develops in a family and is present in several members of the family."(16)

During the midfifties, in addition to the Bateson project on schizophrenia, other research in the same area was being carried on at the National Institute of Mental Health in Bethesda, Maryland, and at Yale University. Under the auspices of NIMH, Lyman Wynne began to publish his results.(17) One of the kinds of relationships frequently observed in his research which was to become important in family therapy he called "pseudomutuality." This is characterized by an intense and stereotyped clinging to the pretense that an ideal family situation exists. At Yale, Theodore Lidz, published a significant article on the transmission of irrationality in schizophrenic families and its relationship to the family environment.(18) In 1958, the late Nathan Ackerman wrote the first full-length study combining theory and practice, in which he emphasized the importance of role relations within the family.(19) Murray Bowen and his associates, most notably Warren Brodey, were also involved in studying schizophrenia.(20) Their findings in general agreed with those of Lidz and Wynne. In brief the evidence for a definite relationship between schizophrenia and the family system was mounting.

In addition to these American studies, two other items are important because of cross-cultural implications. In 1957, John Howells began to study families in Ipswich, England. Howells took a family stance as a starting point:

In family psychiatry a family is not regarded merely as a background to be modified to help the present patient alone. Family psychiatry accepts *the family itself* as *the patient* the presenting member being viewed as a sign of family psychopathology.(21)

What such a stance produced is detailed by Howells in this work and more recently and extensively at the end of the decade 1960–1970.(22) And in 1958, Ronald Laing began a study of schizophrenic families in London at the Tavistock Clinic. The results published in the early 1960s corroborates much of the American work.(23)

As a result of the research done in the 1950s, a series of new terms began to be introduced by those studying family process. Not only "pseudomutuality," and "double bind," alluded to above, but also "rubber fence," "schism and skew," and "mystification," began to appear in the literature. One might ask: Why a new language? Were there not enough technical terms in therapeutic jargon without adding to the list? Indeed there were enough but they were not adequate to the realities being observed. Most of them had come out of studies which focused on one person in a system. When the system itself became the focus, the language proved inadequate. There was need then to invent new terms, however inadequate, to try to describe the new realities.

Note that most of the research mentioned deals with the relationship of a schizophrenic to his family. However, observers also could see similarities between such families and so-called normal ones. In these families the processes that produced such things as "double binds" were present although not as often nor as severe. It was becoming clear that although the subjects observed were frequently severely disturbed, the applications of what was observed could be extended to a much wider range of family. This, in fact, is what happened and how theory in family therapy developed.

AN OVERVIEW OF FAMILY THERAPY

In March 1970, the Group for the Advancement of Psychiatry published a study of family therapy based on a questionnaire issued in 1967. The study is an overview of the field or a snapshot and is by no means exhaustive. However, in one part of the questionnaire, the therapists are asked to name those theorists they regard as most important. Those named in order are Virginia Satir, Nathan Ackerman, Don Jackson, Jay Haley, Murray Bowen. (24)

In a similar study done in 1970, the author sent a questionnaire to family therapists, selected at random, and received the same five names although in a slightly different order. From this it would seem that family therapists are agreed on whose thinking is most seminal in their field (Foley, unpublished dissertation, 1971).

This work is an attempt to examine both the major concepts in family therapy and the key ideas of its leading thinkers. After presenting these notions, I will compare these thinkers along a series of dimensions which will allow us to note similarities and differences. Finally, I will speculate on the future of family therapy based on the material presented.

In addition to an examination of the literature, personal correspondence and interviews have been used to present the reader with a picture of family therapy which depicts the thinking of a theorist and to mitigate the prejudices of the author. Such an approach allows us to get some idea of where family therapy is going. The material which appears in professional journals is necessarily behind the thinking in the field because of the exigencies of publishing. As we move into the mid-seventies, family therapy is making adjustments to a changing society and discarding some old notions and incorporating new ideas. In this book, to chart that course accurately, we must first look at the early conceptualizations made in the 1950s and the modifications in the 1960s.

As Murray Bowen observed:

One of the interesting developments has been the way investigators first conceptualized the system and the ways these concepts have been modified in the past ten years. There were terms for the distortion and rigidity, the reciprocal functioning, and the interlocking, binding, stuck togetherness of the system.[4(p 161)]

Bowen then mentions the double bind, pseudomutuality, and schism and skew as some of the more important concepts arising in the 1950s. To this list, Laing's notion of mystification can be added.

NOTES AND REFERENCES

1. Ackerman N: Family psychotherapy today. Fam. Process 9:123, 1970
2. Olson D: Marital and family therapy: Integrative review and critique. J Marriage Fam 32:501–538, 1970
3. Watzlawick P, Beavin J, Jackson D: Pragmatics of Human Communication. New York, Norton, 1967, p 284
4. Bowen M: The use of family theory in clinical practice, in Haley J (ed): Changing Families. New York, Grune & Stratton, 1971, pp 159–192
5. MacGregor R: Multiple Impact Therapy with Families. New York, McGraw-Hill, 1964
6. Speck R, Attneave C: Family Networks. New York, Pantheon, 1973
7. Laqueur P, Laburt H, Morong, E: Multiple family therapy: Further developments, in Haley J (ed): Changing Families. New York, Grune & Stratton, 1971, pp 82–95
8. Laqueur P: General systems theory: A tool for understanding group therapy—theory and practice. Address given at the annual convention of the American Group Psychotherapy Association, Feb. 8, 1973, Detroit, Michigan
9. Freud S: Analysis of phobia in a five-year-old boy, in Strachey J (ed): The Complete Works of Sigmund Freud, vol. 10. London, Hogarth, 1964, pp 5–148
10. Mead M: The Coming of Age in Samoa. New York, Morrow, 1961, Malinowski B: Sex and Repression in a Savage Society. New York, Meridian Press, 1955.

    These two are among the more prominent contributions of anthropology to an understanding of cultural factors on the individual.
11. Sullivan HS: The Interpersonal Theory of Psychiatry. New York. Norton, 1953

12. Adler A: The Practice and Theory of Individual Psychology. New York, Humanities Press, 1952.
13. Christensen O: Family counseling: An Adlerian orientation, in Gazda G (ed): Proc Symp Fam Couns Ther. Athens, Georgia, Symposium, Winter 1971, Univ. of Georgia, School of Education, pp 15–32.
14. Ruesch J, Bateson G: Communication: The Social Matrix of Society. New York, Norton, 1951
15. Bateson G, Jackson D, Haley J, Weakland J: Toward a theory of schizophrenic, in Jackson D (ed): Communication, Family and Marriage. Palo Alto, Science and Behavior Books, 1968, pp 31–55
16. Midelfort C: The Family in Psychotherapy. New York, McGraw-Hill, 1957, p 192
17. Wynne L, Ryckoff I, Day J, Hirsch S: Pseudomutuality in the family relationship of schizophrenics. Psychiatry 21:1958, 205–220
18. Lidz T, Terry D, Fleck S: The intrafamilial environment of the schizophrenic patient: VI. The transmission of irrationality. Arch Neurol Psychiatry 79: 1958, 305–316
19. Ackerman N: The Psychodynamics of Family Life. New York, Basic Books, 1958
20. Brodey W: Some family operations and schizophrenia. Arch Gen Psychiatr 1:1959, 379–402
21. Howells J: Family Psychiatry, Springfield, Ill., Thomas 1963, pp 4–5
22. Howells J: Theory and Practice of Family Psychiatry. New York, Brunner/Mazel, 1971
23. Laing R, Esterson A: Sanity, Madness, and the Family. Baltimore, Penguin, 1964
24. Group for the advancement of psychiatry. Field Fam Ther. 7 (78): 570, 1970

PART I

Seminal Ideas in Family Therapy

1

The Double Bind

In 1956 Bateson, Jackson, Haley, and Weakland combined forces and produced a paper that has become a classic in family therapy and communication theory.(1) "Toward a Theory of Schizophrenia" combines the thinking of an anthropologist, a psychiatrist, a communications expert, and a researcher who have produced an article of extraordinary richness and value.

Haley recognized that the symptoms of schizophrenia are suggestive of an inability to recognize logical types as conceived by Bertrand Russell. Bateson added to this the notion that the symptoms and etiology of schizophrenia could be formulated in terms of a double bind hypothesis. This hypothesis was similar to Jackson's concept of family homeostasis; that is, the process which enables a family system to maintain its equilibrium. Finally, Weakland and Haley articulated the formal analogies between hypnosis and schizophrenia.(2)

Basically, Jackson and his associates examined the effects of paradox in human interaction. The key to understanding its central concept is the difference between a simple contradiction and a paradox. The former means that one has a choice of doing one thing or another and is a case of either/or. The latter, however, is defined as " . . . a *contradiction that follows correct deduction from consistent premises.*"(3)

Logicians distinguish three types of paradoxes:

1. Antinomies are statements which are contradictory but provable and found in logical and mathematical systems.

2. Semantic antinomies are those arising out of hidden inconsistencies in the level structure of thought and language.
3. Pragmatic paradoxes are divided into paradoxical predictions and paradoxical injunctions. These grow out of antinomies and semantic antinomies and are relevant here because they come out of ongoing interactions and determine behavior. The double bind is an example of a paradoxical injunction.

Bertrand Russell in his theory of logical types holds that whatever involves all of a collection must not be one of the collection. A paradoxical injunction illustrates Russell's thinking. The paradox results from a confusion of levels of meaning. Since a class is a higher type than its members, even to postulate it, one has to go to a higher level in the hierarchy of types. Therefore, and this is the key point, to say that the class of all concepts is itself a concept is not false but meaningless.(4) The difference then between a simple contradiction and a paradoxical injunction (double bind) is that in the former case one can make a choice since choice is possible, but in the latter case no choice is logically possible.

This somewhat abstract and excellent summary of the subtleties of Lord Russell's thought has been translated into a striking example by humorist Dan Greenburg. "Give your son Marvin two sports shirts as a present. The first time he wears one of them look at him sadly and say in your Basic Tone of Voice: 'The other one you didn't like?' " For Marvin no choice is possible.(5)

However, for double binding to take place there must be several conditions present over a period of time. First, there must be two or more persons present, one of whom is designated a "victim." Second, the experience must be reinforced by repetition. Therapists postulate that a single traumatic experience would not be sufficient. Third, a primary negative injunction must be present. Paul Watzlawick sees it as having either of two forms. The victim is told, "Do not do so and so, or I will punish you," or he is told, "If you do not do so and so, I will punish you." Fourth, a secondary injunction conflicting with the first at a more abstract level, and like the first, enforced by punishments or signals which threaten survival. This injunction is commonly communicated on a nonverbal level. Finally, a third negative injunction is imposed, prohibiting the "victim" from escaping from the field. (6)

When these conditions are present over a period of time, therapists postulate that eventually not all need be present to trigger off the "victim." The presence of even one will be sufficient to put the "victim" in a double bind. One obviously is reminded of Pavlov and his experiments. The double bind "victim" like Pavlov's dogs has learned to perceive his world in a structured pattern, and the complete list of ingredients is no longer required to produce a given response.

What is so significant about the double bind is that it is not confined to schizophrenic families alone but occurs in mitigated form in a large number of so-called normal families.

What does the "victim" do in a double bind? Jackson and his associates suggest three possibilities.[3 (pp 217–218)] First, one concludes the "victim" is overlooking something in the situation. He searches and searches but the more he tries to understand, the more confused he becomes. A second possibility is to become absolutely literal and follow each and every injunction to the letter. The basic premise underlying this approach is that things do not make sense anyhow so why worry. Anyone familiar with institutional living, for example, the army, will recognize this response. A third option is to withdraw from human involvement so that all incoming material is blocked out. The "victim" is caught because he cannot discuss the messages with an outside party. He cannot metacommunicate, that is, talk about his communication and thus escape his field. The "victim" therefore remains trapped and unable to escape.

Understanding what is being said requires a context in which the receiver can make sense of what the sender is transmitting. Words alone are not sufficient. Is a message a compliment or a complaint? Is it a way of saying you are loved or hated? The receiver can only know by grasping the context in which the message is sent. Nonverbal clues such as smiles or frowns, and tones of voice indicating warmth or displeasure, give us a context in which we make meaning of what is communicated.

However, the "victim" is unable to grasp the context because it is constantly changing and seems to be saying two different things at the same time. On one level it is saying yes, and on another it is saying no. The "victim," as Jackson suggests, gets caught in the process and endlessly repeats his behavior seeking to find meaning in the messages that are sent to him. When the receiver of such messages cannot comment on the messages received (metacommunication) and when they come from people who are emotionally significant to him for his survival, this creates a problem. If this person, the "victim," is part of a system such as a family, he is in trouble. The creators of the theory of the double bind liken the situation to " ... any self-correcting system which has lost its governor, it spirals into never-ending, but always systematic, distortions."[1 (p 40)]

Outside help in the form of a therapist may be needed to

reconstruct the system of the "victim." How this might be done, the role of feedback, especially positive feedback (that which tends to amplify deviations) is brilliantly described by Lynn Hoffman.(7) An understanding of the elements involved in the double bind enable the student to grasp more clearly what theorists are doing in practice. Hopefully, there is a rational for what the family therapist is doing.

The concept of the double bind is important because it has survived in family therapy and has led to some important developments in the decade following its introduction. Like any good idea the double bind theory has been productive beyond its original conception. The therapist faced with repetitive patterns in a family wonders what he can do to break into the seemingly closed system.

A whole approach to this problem of repetitive patterns, a series of strategies using the induction of crisis into the family system, has been devised by Salvador Minuchin and his associates.(8) Although an examination of this approach is beyond the scope of this book, nevertheless, I mention it because it shows us the connections that exist between theory and practice and how an interplay between them is vital.

In 1959, Bateson, in discussing schizophrenia examines the implications of the double bind theory to this form of psychosis.[2 (pp 244–270)] He finds many and varied implications. The double bind is tied not only into learning as one might suspect but also into genetics. Bateson writes: "If schizophrenia be a modification or distortion of the learning process, then when we ask about the genetics of schizophrenia, we cannot be content just with genealogies upon which we discriminate some individuals who have been committed to hospitals, and others who have not."[2 (p 258)] It is evident that Bateson is interested in an ecological perspective and sees the double bind in this light. Knowledge which has ramification in one field has ramifications in another. The world of the schizophrenic then and the world of the so-called normal may differ but they both share a common world.

In summary, the double bind theory has been modified and changed in the course of time. Bateson says that in its original form it seemed to speak of itself as if it were a "something." This process in which an idea is almost personified is known as *reification*. This is false to the reality but it contains a grain of truth. In its most recent and sophisticated form, the double bind theory "asserts that there is an experiential component in the determination or etiology of schizophrenic symptoms . . . " so that " . . . there is nothing to determine whether a given individual shall become a clown, a poet, a schizophrenic, or some combinations of these."[2 (p 272)]

Bateson suggests that some interplay of genetics and environment is operating in a given situation. He emphasizes the importance of what he calls the "transcontextual" in determining what road a person will follow to enrichment or impoverishment. In any case, Bateson is refining the double bind theory, making it less rigid and objective and seeing it in a context. He is aware that the double bind is not a thing in itself but an expression to describe an interactional process.

Apparently, the double bind concept of the 1970s, seen now not in isolation but in relationship to others ideas, will be with us. It will be with us because ecological factors cannot be ignored. Ecology is central for Bateson and also for Minuchin who feels that unless family therapy moves toward an ecological theory of man, it is doomed to be entombed, to be ossified.(9)

NOTES AND REFERENCES

1. Bateson G, Jackson D, Haley J, Weakland J: Toward a theory of schizophrenia, in Jackson D (ed): Communication, Family, and Marriage. Palo Alto, Science & Behavior Books, 1968, pp 31–55
2. Bateson G: Steps to an Ecology of Mind. New York, Ballantine Books, 1972, p 202
3. Watzlawick P, Beavin J, Jackson D: Pragmatics of Human Communication. New York, Norton, 1967, p 188
4. Whitehead A, Russell B: Principia Mathematica. New York, Norton, 1938
5. Greenburg D: How to Be a Jewish Mother. Los Angeles, Price, Sloan & Stern, 1964, p 16
6. Watzlawick P: A review of the double bind theory, in Jackson D (ed): Communication, Family, and Marriage. Palo Alto, Science & Behavior Books, 1968, p 64
7. Hoffman L: Deviation-amplifying processes in natural groups, in Haley J (ed): Changing Families. New York, Grune & Stratton, 1971, pp 285–311
8. Minuchin S, Barcai A: Therapeutically induced family crisis, in Masserman J (ed): Science and Psychoanalysis, Childhood and Adolescence vol. 14. New York, Grune & Stratton, 1969, pp 199–205
9. Minuchin S: Family therapy: Technique or theory? In Masserman J (ed): Science and Psychoanalysis, vol. 14. New York, Grune & Stratton, 1969, pp 179–187

Also Chapter 12 of this book.

2

Pseudomutuality and Pseudohostility

PSEUDOMUTUALITY

These two concepts can be put together because they have been investigated and articulated by a team of researchers associated with Lyman Wynne and Margaret Singer. The concept of pseudomutuality, first introduced by Wynne in 1958, developed throughout the following decade. Additional work done in the 1960s on the thought patterns of schizophrenics produced some refinements. Along with this research Wynne and his associates were also incorporating their findings into therapeutic strategies devised to deal with family systems.

The body of research then coming out of the NIMH has been among the more prominent in the development of family therapy and constitutes an important part of its history. Wynne, who has been interested in the family as a whole from the very beginning of his work, writes:

> The purpose of this paper is to develop a psychodynamic interpretation of schizophrenia that takes into conceptual account the social organization of the family as a whole.(1)

A person seems to have two needs which bring him into conflict. On the one hand, he has a need to develop a sense of personal identity, and on the other, a need to relate to others. In terms of the family, the former need is centrifugal driving one outside its boundaries and is involved in the important psychic process of separation. The latter need, however, is centripetal driving a person back into the family system and is involved with the psychic process of striving for closeness.

In a healthily functioning person these two needs are balanced. One is able to relate to others, to get close, and does not lose his sense of self and become absorbed in the other. He can move within the family system and can be himself. In a person who is having difficulty in functioning, however, a situation exists in which the person is often uncertain about his boundaries, and he has a real fear of losing his identity.

What is valuable in Wynne's contribution to family therapy is that he saw this dilemma within the wider context of the family and did not limit himself only to the individual patient. His insight is that he wished to study schizophrenia from the point of view of the social organization of the family. He asks in what way is the family involved in the manner a schizophrenic puts his world together? Does it play a role, or not? If so, is it a major or minor role?

Wynne begins with a description of identity and says that it is the feeling about self that remains coherent despite the constant flux of stimuli. Identity means that although the world is changing and everything in it, some people have the ability to use the term "I" in an ongoing fashion, whereas others do not. In addition, some people have a stronger sense of their "I" than others. Finally, living in a family system seems to strengthen the "I" in some and weaken it in others. Wynne focuses on this last dimension. He inquires how one can remain one's self and fulfill one's need for self-identity, and yet fulfill his need to relate to significant others. How can he maintain a balance? What are the options?

Wynne feels there are three options: (1) Mutuality, which is characterized by a divergence of self-interests; (2) Nonmutuality, which is found, for example, in the relationship of a customer and a sales clerk; (3) Pseudomutuality, which is "a predominant absorption in fitting together at the expense of the differentiation of the identities of the persons in the relation."[1 (p 207)]

It follows from this that an affirmation of a sense of personal identity is seen as a threat to the whole system of the family. We should note that much of Wynne's thinking has been influenced by the concepts of Parsons and Bales who see the family as a social subsystem. When viewed in this way, there is a strong emphasis on the concept of role, its expression and delineation. As Wynne sees it, any family, but especially a schizophrenic one, gets locked into roles and finds it almost impossible to escape. The sicker the family, the more rigid the roles.

Wynne states that family pseudomutuality is characterized by four qualities:

1. Sameness of role structure,
2. Insistence on desirability and appropriateness of this role structure,
3. Intense concern over independence from this role structure,
4. Absence of spontaneity, humor, and zest.

The family, therefore, becomes not only the center or focus of life but also the totality of it. The outreach of the family is complete and encompasses all aspects of life since " . . . the family role structure is experienced as all-encompassing."[1 (211)]

To explain this flexible family boundary, Wynne and his associates coined the felicitous expression "a rubber fence." They see the family as being able to stretch its boundaries to include those things which are complementary and to contract to exclude those that are noncomplementary.

Because of its all-encompassing bounds, the person in such a family cannot trust his own perceptions, and is therefore unable to escape, since the walls around him expand and contract but never remain fixed. The rules of the game are constantly changing and a player never knows what they are. An interplay of indiscriminate approval and secrecy keeps the person in a constant state of confusion.

The schizophrenic then, in his own opinion, has problems of identity, perception, and communication because of the way in which the family is organized as a social system. Wynne is suggesting that schizophrenia is not just an entity associated with certain clinical personalities but is caused by the manner in which a person is socialized. He summarizes the concept of pseudomutual complementarity as "a new extension of role theory which takes into account the quality of subjective experience of the person taking a role."[1 (220)]

In 1959, Wynne and his associates examined the concept of roles and identity further.(2) Wynne feels that in the development of personality, there is an unknown, an X quality. One must learn a role and identify with significant others to be sure but this is not enough to form a sense of identity. Wynne postulates a jump from these to identity and feels that the schizophrenic cannot make this jump. "It is precisely this big jump, from roles and identification to identity that the schizophrenic fails to make."[2 (94)] And he fails to make it not by his own fault alone but because of the family structure. Any attempt to change the rigidly defined family role must deal with the powerful, repressive forces at work in the family.

The importance of role relations described here had first been spelled out in 1957. Wynne at the time was investigating the role of siblings in a family. In his study of monozygotic quadruplet schizophrenics, he concludes that the psychological meaning built up from nonspecific physical characteristics may contribute to differing role definitions for siblings within the same family.(3)
Wynne's contribution has been to see schizophrenia in terms of the family system. All are part of the system and there are no victims strictly so-called. Wynne observes:

Therapists tend to perceive the family's difficulties as located in the parents.(4)
Again and again, when observing such sequences in family therapy, we have been impressed with the oversimplification contained in the idea that the schizophrenic child is the "victim" of "schizophrenogenic" parents. Rather, all family members, offspring and parents, are caught up in reciprocal victimizing—and rescuing—processes in which they are all tragically enmeshed.[4 (p 112)]

PSEUDOHOSTILITY

Having introduced the concept of pseudomutuality Wynne developed one of pseudohostility. This concept refers to a split or alienation which remains limited to a surface level. Beneath that surface, Wynne suggests pseudohostility like its counterpart, pseudomutuality, covers a need for intimacy and affection as well as the more obvious destructive element. Dynamically, pseudohostility and pseudomutuality are very close. They both cover more positive aspects and feelings which seem to get conveyed in diffuse ways.

The two terms are ways of dealing with the observable phenomenon of alignments and splits that exist in families. An alignment is defined as the experience of common interest, attitude, or set of values among two or more persons in the family. A split is the comparable experience of opposition, estrangement and difference. A combination of the two tells us the kind of emotional system we have. Clearly, this is an application of a system approach.[4 (pp 96–97)]
From 1963 to 1965, Wynne and Singer produced a series of four articles in which they examined the relationship between thought disorders and certain kinds of families. More precisely, the study was an attempt to examine the interplay of biological variations and family role expectation, together with societal role expectations. In the study they developed some fundamental notions found in the 1958 article on pseudomutuality. At that time, Wynne proposed a hypothesis that the

fragmentation of experience, the identity diffusion, and the disturbed modes of perception and communication found in the acute reactive schizophrenic's personality structure are to a significant extent derived from processes of internalization from characteristics of the family social organization.

Two clear observations come from the study. First, the overtly schizophrenic member becomes more deeply enmeshed in the family's emotional life than the nonschizophrenic; and second, such people usually fill conflicted roles in the family.(5) Again, we can observe that it is not a question of one member's sickness but rather a question of a sick system in which the identified client is only the most prominent member. Also, roles tend to get fixed in such families and do not change. There is established a pattern of rigidity which cannot allow for change in role expectation.

In the same issue, Singer and Wynne introduce the differentiation–integration principle. This maintains that whenever development occurs, it proceeds from a state of lack of differentiation to a state of differentiation, articulation, and hierarchic integration.(6) A quality of "stuck togetherness' is noted. The lines of demarcation that separate people from one another and set them apart are missing in these families. Wynne and Singer suggest that, in part, the inability to accomplish the process of differentiation accounts for the thinking disorders in identified schizophrenics. Such patterns are not wholly personal and idiosyncratic but, in part, learned responses.

Since thinking disorders are viewed along a continuum, they feel distinctions of disorganization can be made. They speak of amorphousness, that is, global, undifferentiated forms of functioning and fragmentation, or a failure of hierarchic integration. Two years later Singer and Wynne carried the ability to make distinctions in thinking a step further and developed it into a methodology of predicting. The procedure was to administer projective tests to the nonschizophrenic members of the family, and on the basis of the results obtained, to predict the form of thinking and the degree of disorganization of the patient. The tester (Margaret Singer) would blindly match patients and their families.(7)

Singer obtained an unusually high correlation in testing the families and their members. The investigators note that four family features arise from the results:

1.   Styles of communicating. These range from amorphous to borderline. What is most significant is the manner in which the patterns of attention are handled.

2. Styles of relating. An all or nothing at all type of relating was found. The distance and closeness tended to be erratic and inappropriate.
3. Affective disorders. Underlying feelings of pervasive meaningless-ness and emptiness were uncovered.
4. Overall structure of the family. Pseudomutuality and pseudohostil-ity were characteristic of the families.

Although these tests were made on schizophrenic families, the investigators would insist that what can be said in these cases can be said also for so-called normal families. The concepts of pseudomutual-ity and pseudohostility, therefore, are not limited to families of schizophrenics.

In the fourth article in the series Singer and Wynne summarize the insights gained and also elaborate on the methods used to obtain the data. Two points are worth noting. First, the approach to the research is similar to that of a general system theory. Second, the method used was a transactional point of view.(8)

The Wynne-Singer research is regarded as important not only for the results obtained but for a shift from the person to the family, from the intrapsychic to the interpersonal, from a linear cause–effect to a circular mutual causality. Perhaps the best summary of Wynne's research is found in the statement that within the culture of the schizophrenic family there is a governing assumption, namely, nothing has a meaningful relation to anything else.(9)

Nothing is in its proper place since there seems to be no proper place. Relationship is either nonexistent or nonmeaningful. Roles are either rigidly patterned or vague and amorphous. The outsider cannot get inside the family structure precisely because there is no family structure but an almost boundless "rubber fence." Morris and Wynne use excerpts from conjoint family sessions to illustrate the points made above. They evaluate the material along three lines:

1. Parental styles of handling attention and developing meaning especially the context,
2. Family role structure,
3. Parental styles of expressing affect.(10)

The links between schizophrenic disorders in a person and his family's method of socialization are delineated. In addition, the potential value of a predictive method in psychiatric research is seen.

IMPORTANCE OF WYNNE'S RESEARCH

First of all, Wynne opted for a family approach to schizophrenia. He maintained that pathology was not found alone in a person but was in the family system. Second, the importance of role relations within the family was emphasized. The family was seen as a "social subsystem" as conceived in the thinking of Parsons and Bales. One of the goals or outcomes of family therapy for Wynne is a "delineation of roles." More specifically Wynne proposed that a loosening of roles in the family if they are too rigid, or a clarification of them if too vague.

Third, communicational patterns and pathology are stressed. It is through communication that roles get spelled out so that a confused or distorted picture of role is necessarily linked to communication. Finally, the concepts of "pseudomutuality," and "rubber fence" were introduced. These notions have proved to be among the key concepts in family process. They were early attempts to characterize what goes on in a relationship system. Individual theory did not offer an adequate conceptual model so investigators like Wynne had to coin phrases to describe the kinds of phenomena they met in families.

Because of Wynne's research, other therapists began to move away from individual models toward interactional ones. During the late 1950s there was an effort to create new ways of viewing family pathology. Clinicians could observe interaction, but they did not have an adequate terminology to describe it. Wynne's concepts of "pseudomutuality," "pseudohostility," and the "rubber fence" were all significant steps in the creation of a new way of viewing family process. Wynne has kept a flexibility in this thinking which is rare. He is continuously revising his ideas and how they may be more effectively applied to family therapy. In 1965, he published a paper on the indications and contraindications for family therapy.(11)

In 1970, he revised the earlier paper to bring it into line with his later concepts.(12) "I do not regard the method of family therapy as a psychiatric panacea—not as applicable to all varieties of psychiatric difficulties—but as a valuable ingredient in a comprehensive psychiatric repertory."[12 (pp 96–97)] This is a refreshing statement to read and shows a willingness to listen and be open-minded.

Wynne has tried to relate his practice to his theory. He is not only a clinician but a researcher. The indications for family therapy as well as the contraindications are based on his research. Over the years he had added and subtracted from his approach with utmost care. His value then to family therapy is not only his research work but the caution with which it is applied. If family therapy is to grow in the

1970s, it is necessary for the field to emulate Wynne's example of combining theory and practice so that practice is based on observation and theory is nourished by contact with patients.

REFERENCES

1. Wynne L, Ryckoff I, Day J, Hirsch S: Pseudomutuality in the family relations of schizophrenics. Psychiatry 21: 205, 1958
2. Ryckoff I, Day J, Wynne L: Maintenance of stereotyped roles in families of schizophrenics. Arch Gen Psychiatry I: 93–98, 1959
3. Wynne L: Family relations of a set of monozygotic quadruplet schizophrenics. Orell Fuscli Arts Graphiques 2: 43–49, 1957
4. Wynne L: The study of intrafamilial alignments and splits in exploratory family therapy, in Ackerman N, Beatman F, Sherman S (eds): Exploring the Base for Family Therapy. New York, Family Service, 1961, p 103
5. Wynne L, Singer M: Thought disorder and family relations of schizophrenics: I. Research strategy. Arch Gen Psychiatry 9:191–198, 1963
6. Singer M, Wynne L: Thought disorder and family relations of schizophrenics: II. Classification of forms of thinking. Arch Gen Psychiatry 9:199–206, 1963
7. Singer M, Wynne L: Thought disorder and family relations of schizophrenics: III. Methodology using projective techniques. Arch Gen Psychiatry 12:187–200, 1965
8. Singer M, Wynne L: Thought disorder and family relations of schizophrenics: IV. Results and Implications. Arch Gen Psychiatry 12:201–212, 1965
9. Schaffer L, Wynne L, Day J, Ryckoff I, Halperin A: On the nature and sources of the psychiatric experience with the family of the schizophrenic. Psychiatry 25:44, 1962
10. Morris G, Wynne L: Schizophrenic offspring and parental styles of communications: Predictive study using family therapy excerpts. Psychiatry 28:32–39, 1965
11. Wynne L: Some indications and contraindications for exploratory family therapy, in Boszormenyi-Nagy I, Framo, J (eds): Intensive Family Therapy. New York, Harper & Row, 1965, pp 289–322
12. Wynne L: Some guidelines for exploratory conjoint family therapy, in Haley J (ed): Changing Families. New York, Grune & Stratton, 1971 pp 96–115

3

Schism and Skew

In the mid-fifties, Lidz and his associates at Yale University began a long and careful investigation of the relationship between schizophrenia and the family. What is significant about his research is that his conclusions are so similar to those of Wynne and his associates. Lidz observed general patterns of difficulty which seem to occur regularly in the relationship between the schizophrenic and his family. Among these patterns he sees three general areas of difficulty:

1. Deficiencies of paternal nurturance. This lack resulted in the patient's failure to achieve autonomy and an inability to function in a self-reliant way;
2. The failure of the family as a social institution, especially in its inability to provide the patient with adequate role models;
3. Failure to transmit the communicative and other basic instrumental techniques of the culture to the child.(1)

Lidz maintains that both a mother and a father are necessary if a child is to grow up in a reasonably successful way. A child must have a member of the same sex to identify with, and a member of the opposite sex who is seen as desirable. When the parents are divided and quarreling, the child cannot achieve this twofold goal. This cooperation between father and mother Lidz calls the parental coalition. It occurs when both are able to fulfill their respective roles as man and woman and as husband and wife.

In addition to the parental coalition, Lidz says that there must be a maintenance of generational boundaries between parents and children. He says that for the child's normal development, he must know that he cannot take one parent's place with the other, and that although he may identify with a parent, he does not become a parent figure in the familial home. Finally, there must be a maintenance also of sex-linked roles.(2) In this Lidz is following the ideas set forth by Parsons and Bales.(3)

Parsons and Bales state that the father is the instrumental leader of the family, and the mother the expressive-affectional leader. Lidz finds that unless the parents have a clear-cut understanding of their own sexual roles, the child becomes confused. Sexual identity is not just a matter of biology but is linked to a conception of role in the family. In schizophrenic families, there is serious confusion regarding roles, however, it is noted in less disturbed but pained families, as well.

From this we can readily see that Lidz would hold that the relationship of the father and mother is the crucial one in the family. Again, in his studies he finds that in families with a schizophrenic child, the marital relationship is disturbed in one of two directions.

SCHISM AND SKEW

Some marriages are either marked by a chronic failure to achieve a complementarity of purpose or role reciprocity or marked by excessive attachment to the parental home. Lidz labels such unions as marital schisms. Other marriages are characterized by one strong and one weak partner. In these unions the weak partner allows the stronger to dominate the relationship. These marriages are said to be skewed.

Lidz observes that the absence of role reciprocity means constant tension. This confusion gets transmitted through the course of time to the children. As a result there is a confusion of identity. The importance of Lidz's research to family therapy is not in specific approaches or techniques but in his way of thinking about the relationship of the familial system. As Lidz explains:

The approach that I have taken considers personality development from the perspective of the family matrix, considering the child as the member of a group entity in which the behavior of one member affects all.[2 (p 589)]

To understand the family matrix more closely it is necessary to look at the roles of the father and mother in the family process. Lidz's studies reveal that the father plays an essential role in the development of the child. Although this might seem almost self-evident, nevertheless, many of the early studies of family problems tended to neglect the role of the father.

Lidz finds clinical evidence to support the theoretical position of Parsons and Bales that the father is the adaptive-instrumental leader. He states that a "weak, ineffectual father" is more destructive than a "cold, unyielding one" because in our culture a weak ineffectual father would provide a maladaptive image for the growing child. Following the traditional psychoanalytic analysis of personality development, Lidz states that with a weak, ineffectual father present, it would be very difficult for a child of either sex to have a successful outcome of the oedipal phase.

Finally, Lidz describes many of the fathers he has studied as having an imperviousness to the feelings and needs of others. It is this imperviousness, spelled out in different ways, which contributes one essential part to the building of problems within the family. The other, of course, is the mother. The mother, as stated previously, is the affective leader of the family. More specifically, Lidz feels that there are three components to mothering.

First, there is a maternal nurturant relationship. The mother must see the child almost as an extension of herself. The mother must feel a warmth toward her child, but this becomes difficult unless she has experienced this in her own life. As the child grows, it is necessary for the mother to allow the child to separate himself from her. Again, the relationship with the husband is crucial. The "loss of the child" can be compensated for if the husband is warm and affectionate to the wife. In the absence of this, the mother finds it increasingly difficult to allow the child the freedom he needs.

A second requirement is the woman's ability to play her part in the family structure, that is, to form the parental coalition, to keep the generational boundaries and to fulfill her sex-linked role. In line with findings about the father and his role in the family, Lidz states that the "cold, unyielding" mother is more destructive than a "cold, unyielding" father. This is so because of the specific affectional role she plays in the family picture.

Third, the mother is the prime teacher of the instrumental techniques of the culture. The learning of language and its associated transmission of the values of society rests primarily with the mother. Most of these values are shared with the child in ways that are not verbal. Moreover, communication is constantly going on between parent and child.

It is obvious then, that both parents have interlocking roles to play in the process of educating children emotionally. It is likewise clear

that a failure of one parent results in a disturbance in the delicate
marital balance of the system and frequently results in disturbed
children.

Two final questions remain. How do problems get transmitted
through the family system? How do the children become infected with
the contagion of emotional distress? Lidz proposes two closely related
hypotheses: the rationality of the parents and the nature of communication within the family.

The rationality of the parents is at best tenuous. Fact and opinion
are easily mixed up. There is the rigidity of thinking which characterizes all people in distress. Lidz comments, "They (the children) live in a
Procrustean environment, in which events are distorted to fit the mold.
. . . The environment affords training in irrationality." [1 (p 180)]

The process is constant and total. Irrational communication is
transmitted not only in words but also nonverbally. "The family is the
primary teacher of social interaction and emotional reactivity. It
teaches by means of its milieu and nonverbal communication more
than by formal education."[1 (p 174)] It is this last finding, that is, the
role of communication, which other family theorists, notably Jackson
and Satir, will develop at length as we shall see.

IMPORTANCE OF LIDZ'S RESEARCH

First, Lidz sees the relationship of a family as an ongoing,
developmental process. He does not view pathology as an isolated
phenomenon found in the identified client alone. This in itself was an
important step in family therapy. It is cited by Jackson and Satir as one
of the highlights of the acceptance of the role of the family in the
process of schizophrenia.(4)

Second, Lidz sees within the person room for either growth or
decline. He says there are two factors constantly at work and
interacting: the genetic endowment of a person and the effect of his
culture.(5) Such an approach is a move away from the biological model
of health or sickness which left little room for nongenetic factors.

Third, schizophrenia is not inevitable. It is "a possibility inherent
in the developmental process."[5 (22)] Moreover, the family is the
matrix out of which this growth or decline comes. From his studies in
schizophrenia, Lidz has formulated an approach which places the
cause of pathology in the family and not in the individual member. This
is one of the foundations of family therapy agreed on by all theorists of
whatever school and formulated, in part, out of Lidz's research.

Finally, Lidz's research on the importance of symbolic functioning had a direct influence on the work of the communication theorists.
Moreover, the independent research of Wynne and Singer on communication patterns tended to support the findings of Lidz. In addition,
Singer worked with protocols supplied by Lidz, and as a result further
research was begun on the relationship between parental styles of
thinking and the offspring's thought disorder. The area then of thought
disorders and communication has become one of the best researched
in the field of schzophrenia and has been extended to other areas as
well.

Although Lidz's original work was with schizophrenic families, he
feels that the results can be extended to other families and are not
limited. By concentrating on the family as a unit, Lidz has uncovered
structural elements which he feels are relevant in the study of
personality:

But our studies go beyond the intrafamilial object relations taken in a
strict sense and focus also upon the influences of the family as a unit, in order
to examine the structural requisites of the family that are essential to the
promotion of integral ego structure in its offspring. The material derived from
the study indicates that neglect of these structural essentials may be a major
shortcoming in current approaches to the study of personality development.(6)

In summary, we can say that Lidz made several significant
contributions to the field of family therapy. First, his research revealed
the importance of the family system in the development of pathology.
Second, the importance of disturbed communication patterns within
the family were emphasized as observable in the pathology of the
system. In addition, Lidz added his weight to the side of those who
were stressing the importance of the family in the development of
schizophrenia. His research helped build the case for the importance
of the role of the family in its development.

The concepts of schism and skew, like those of the double bind
and pseudomutuality, became part of the language of family therapy
and they survived. They survived because they applied not only to
schizophrenics and their families but to so-called normal families, as
well. The research then of Lidz and his associates, like that of
Bateson, Wynne, and their associates, produced a significant and
important body of knowledge that was widely applicable. Its value is
shown in its survival and its usefulness to the family therapist.

At about the same time that this research in America was going on,
in England, Ronald Laing was looking into similar relationships. As we
shall now see, starting with different ways of conceptualizing family

interaction and with a different kind of client, Laing arrived at conclusions about the schizophrenic and his family that closely approximate the American research.

NOTES AND REFERENCES

1. Lidz T, Fleck S: Family studies and a theory of schizophrenia, in Lidz T, Fleck S, Cornelison, A (eds): Schizophrenia and the Family. New York, International Univ. Press, 1965, pp 362–372
2. Lidz T: Family organization and personality structure, in Bell N, Vogel E (eds): A Modern Introduction to the Family. New York, Free Press, 1968, p 585
3. Parsons T: The incest taboo in relation to social structure and the socialization of the child. Br J Sociol 5: 101–117, 1954

    This article shows how extensive Freudian psychodynamics have been in the thinking of Parsons.

    Also Parsons T, Bales R: Family, Socialization, and Interaction Process. New York, Free Press, 1955
4. Jackson D, Satir V: A review of psychiatric developments in family diagnosis and family therapy, in Ackerman N, Beatman F, Sherman S (eds): Exploring the Base for Family Therapy. New York, Family Service, 1961, p 40
5. Lidz T: Schizophrenia and the family. Psychiatry 21:21–27, 1958
6. Lidz T, Fleck S: Schizophrenia, human integration and the role of the family, in Jackson D (ed): The Etiology of Schizophrenia. New York, Basic Books, 1960, p 330

4

Mystification

In 1958, Ronald Laing and Aaron Esterson began an investigation into the families of schizophrenics in London, which led to the publication of *Sanity, Madness and the Family*.(1) The book is valuable for a number of reasons. It is important because of cross-cultural implications. The families Laing studied came from a different social environment than those studied by Wynne or Lidz. Nevertheless, the kinds of interaction perceived and the types of communication noted bear a striking resemblance to the American studies as noted previously.

In addition, Laing's phenomenological research produces a different kind of observation precisely because he brings a different point of view. He is highly critical, for example, of the value judgments he finds in the work of Lidz.(2) He finds Lidz's concept of the parental coalition to be too cloying and one that robs human life of the possibility of tragedy. Laing further criticizes Lidz's conception of the role of the father in the family: "What is most revealing is the husband's function. The provision of economic support, status, and protection, in that order."[2 (pp 63–64)] Laing is arguing that Lidz's thinking, that of an upper-middle class American, applies perhaps to that group but not to all classes. This is the meaning of his remark that Lidz lists economic support first in priority as the husband's chief concern. In other words, Laing feels that Lidz's thinking is too culturally conditioned. Nevertheless, Laing's research will produce results very similar to those of Lidz. Therefore, despite strong differences in outlook, the two men will find many similarities in their conclusions.

Laing's philosophical debt to Existentialism, especially that of Jean Paul Sartre, shines through clearly in all of his writings.(3) Surely Laing's frame of reference is quite different from that of Lidz. Yet much of the final results of his research are similar to those of Lidz and this is most significant. What is important then is to observe that starting with very different viewpoints and different orientations, both men uncover material so similar.

In the preface to *Sanity, Madness, and the Family*, Laing states that he did not start out to show that the "family is a pathogenic variable in the genesis of schizophrenia."[1 (p 12)] What the material does illustrate is that some behavior which seems socially senseless when viewed apart from family interaction makes more sense when viewed within a family framework.

CONCEPTS OF PRAXIS AND PROCESS

Laing operates exclusively within an interpersonal context. Behavior has no meaning apart from the action and interaction of the people involved. Laing uses the Sartrean concepts of praxis and process. The events, occurrences, and happenings done by doers are termed *praxis.* Those not attributable to an agent are called *process.* Intelligibility, Laing maintains, will result if one can retrace the steps from " . . . what is going on (process) to who is doing what (praxis)." Laing also asks the question: " . . . to what extent is the experience and behavior of that person who has already begun a career as a 'diagnosed' schizophrenic patient intelligible in the light of the praxis and process of his or her family nexus?"[1 (p 27)]

Laing then studies 11 families in the light of this question. He finds, for example, among the Abbotts that the schizophrenic daughter Maya felt she could not express any spontaneous affection for her parents because this was not part of "fitting in." When Maya told them certain things, for example, she had sexual thoughts and she masturbated, the parents told her firmly she did not.[1 (p 42)] Such a repeated pattern made Maya begin to doubt the validity of her own thoughts and feelings. The experience of the world she felt never was corroborated by significant others. Maya, subjected to this kind of interaction, withdrew into her own world.

The Blairs too had a schizophrenic daughter Lucie. Laing observed that she, like Maya, had difficult in seeing herself, except as her father or mother saw her. The family was all encompassing:

However, it was difficult to make any direct relations with others outside the family. The way she saw them, how she thought they saw her, and how she saw herself, were all equally mediated by her father, backed up by her mother.[1 (p 62)]

The seemingly elastic boundaries that Laing notes are part of a process he calls mystification. Not only are Maya and Lucie "mystified" but also Ruby Eden, Jean Head, and Agnes Lawson, as well.

MYSTIFICATION AND ONTOLOGICAL SECURITY

Mystification is the guiding concept of Laing's interpersonal approach. In analyzing it, he describes mystification as the action of one person on another.(4) It is a transpersonal concept and not something going on within a person. Laing defines mystification as "The one person (p) seeks to induce in the other some change necessary for his (p's) security."[4 (p 349)] Mystification, then, is a highly manipulative maneuver which occurs with great frequency in the family life of schizophrenics. Laing feels the function of mystification seems to be "to maintain the status quo."

The more rigid the family structure the more need there is to maintain control of the members of the family. This seems true with families whether found in London, Bethesda, or New Haven. Laing's concept of mystification validates some of the ideas of Harold Searles on driving a person crazy.(5)

Searles talks about three ways or modes used to drive a person crazy:

1.   Stimulation—frustration of same,
2.   Dealing on two unrelated levels of relatedness simultaneously,
3.   Switching from one emotional wave/length to another suddenly.

Laing's analysis of the 11 families bears ample testimony to the constant use of any and all of these modes. The use of these techniques, Laing observes, is not just like a brainwashing in which the goal is to replace one ideology with another. It is more destructive than this since it literally drives a person crazy. The result of the process of mystification is to confuse by means of interpersonal action which is repeated. In time this " ... makes it difficult for the one person to know 'who' the other is, and what is the situation they are 'in.' He does not know 'where he is' any more."(6)

The notion of mystification is connected with, and a development of, an earlier idea, namely, ontological insecurity. Laing's first book

The Divided Self is significantly subtitled *An Existential Study in Sanity and Madness.* By existential, he means the bedrock out of which personality grows. To put it another way: Laing wants to know how a person comes to have a secure sense of himself, and more importantly, what causes a person to become insecure in his grasp of self. The ontologically secure person has a grasp of his own self and of his presence in the world. He is alive and real, and a continuous person in a temporal sense. Laing refers to such a person as an " . . . embodied self having . . . a sense of being flesh and blood and bones, of being biologically alive and real; he knows himself to be substantial."[6 (p 67)]

One who has attained this kind of security of personality finds relationship with others potentially gratifying. However, one who suffers from ontological insecurity is fearful of others because they pose a threat to his own self-possession. Laing proposes three specific forms of anxiety threatening the insecure person: engulfment, implosion, and petrification and depersonalization.

ANXIETY: THREE FORMS

Engulfment is the term Laing uses to describe the person who lacks a clear and strong sense of autonomy. Since a firm sense of one's own autonomous identity is required so that one may be related as one human being to another, the person with vague or weak ego boundaries is constantly afraid of being swallowed up by the other, of being engulfed. Such a person fights constantly to stay afloat emotionally. There are only two poles for him: absorption in the other (engulfment) and complete aloneness (isolation). There is no viable third way of relating or functioning.

Implosion refers to the empty feeling experienced by the ontologically insecure person. Laing likens the experience to the terrible fear that the world will crash in on self and wipe out all identity like gas rushing in to fill up a vacuum. Consequently, any contact with reality is dreaded because it is necessarily implosive by nature and therefore to be feared.

There is also petrification and depersonalization. *Petrification* is taken in its literal sense of fear of being turned to stone. In this case, the person fears being turned from a live person into a robot or automaton. *Depersonalization* is accomplished by not responding to feelings and reducing another into a thing. The ontologically insecure person fears that any kind of relationship will impoverish him. Laing says that these concepts are illustrated in one of his clients, James, who complains that "I am only a response to other people, I have no identity of my own."[6 (p 47)]

The process by which one becomes ontologically insecure is not an intrapsychic one but, as noted above, a transpersonal one. Mystification can be seen as the manner or way in which a person becomes more and more insecure in his own sense of self-identity. Laing's importance conceptually is seen in his insight into the impact of the interpersonal and especially in the role of the family in mystification.

Laing calls the relationship that goes on between people *interexperience*. He defines it as " . . . your behavior and my behavior as I experience it, and your and my behavior as you experience it."[2 (p 19)]

An intrapsychic approach, when talking about persons, is inconceivable since the self only exists in relation to others. This is an axiom of Laing's thinking. "In a science of persons, I shall state as axiomatic that behavior is a function of experience; and both experience and behavior are always in relation to someone or something other than self."[2 (p 25)]

Note, at least in passing, that Laing has become very much involved in the impact of politics on human interaction. In Chapter Three of *The Politics of Experience*, Laing analyzes, at length, the process of mystification used by governments to justify some of the destructive things they do. In his most recent work, *Knots*, Laing further develops the idea of mystification, ontological insecurity, and interexperience in a highly original and poetic manner.(7)

IMPORTANCE OF LAING'S RESEARCH

First, Laing has confirmed some of the theoretical notions of Lidz, Wynne, and the communication theorists and has done so across cross-cultural lines.(8) Not only are Laing's families different geographically from those studied by Lidz and Wynne but also economically and socially, as well.

Second, Laing takes an existential, phenomenological viewpoint of interaction between people. He brings a different frame of reference and yet produces conclusions much like those of the American researchers. One might argue from this that the theoretical stance of the therapist does not noticeable change the results obtained, and consequently, leads one to feel that a family approach gives valid insights. Ideologically, Lidz and Laing are poles apart. Nevertheless, their conclusions are strikingly similar.

Third, and Laing's most important theoretical contribution, is his study of the family nexus of the schizophrenic in the light of praxis and process. This shift from the person to the interpersonal is not just another way of viewing pathology but, as Jay Haley will argue, a totally new and different concept of pathology, demanding new theoretical models and concepts. Laing is just as firm as Haley in his conviction that a family viewpoint is truly revolutionary:

> We believe that the shift of point of view that these descriptions both embody and demand has a historical significance no less radical than the shift from a demonological to a clinical viewpoint three hundred years ago.[1 (p 27)]

The concepts of phenomenology and existentialism are quite foreign to the pragmatic American mind. Reading Laing is more like reading Graham Greene than the study of a psychiatrist and his research. His frame of reference resembles more of a cafe on the Left Bank than the antiseptic walls of a psychiatric institution. It is precisely this difference which is of value. Ideologically, Laing is a rebel. He is against the establishment be it psychiatric, political, or national. Yet, his families and those of Lidz and Wynne are many times interchangeable. The similarities are more real than the differences. Like the Americans, Laing, too, struggled with the interactions he noted and the limitations of language to capture that interaction. The concept of mystification like that of pseudomutuality and schism and skew was born of a need to create some expression which would approximate the complex pattern that goes on in families. Mystification has become part of the language of family therapy because it has expressed an interactional phenomenon that is valid in all families and not just those of schizophrenics. It is of value because it gives the therapist a handle which allows him to deal more effectively with families. It has survived not just as a piece of history but as a concept which has clinical and therefore pragmatic value.

NOTES AND REFERENCES

1. Laing R, Esterson A: Sanity, Madness, and the Family. Baltimore, Penguin, 1964
2. Laing, R: The Politics of Experience. New York, Ballantine, 1967, pp 63–67
3. Laing R, Cooper D: Reason and Violence. A Decade of Sartre's Philosophy 1950–1960. London, Tavistock, 1964

4. Laing R: Mystification, confusion, and conflict, in Boszormenyi-Nagy, I, Framo, J (eds): Intensive Family Therapy. New York, Harper & Row, 1965, pp 343–363
5. Searles H: The effort to drive the other person crazy—an element in the aetiology and psychotherapy of schizophrenia. Br J Med Psychol 32:1–18, 1959
6. Laing, R: The Divided Self. Baltimore, Penguin, 1969, p 122
7. Laing R: Knots. New York, Pantheon, 1970
8. Laing R: The Self and Others. New York, Pantheon, 1969, pp 125–131

Here Laing gives an interesting analysis of the double bind theory.

5

General System Theory

So far in our study we have looked at four concepts that grew out of research with schizophrenics and their families. These notions have had value and have become part of family therapy because they have proved to be viable ways of handling the interactions of even so-called normal families. We now come to a concept that is not derived from clinical data nor even from the field of mental health. However, it is by far the most important concept in family therapy, and the one which dominates the field at present. It is called the *general system theory.*

Family therapy as an approach to the problems of an individual member focuses on the relationship of the person and his family system. This is seen as critical in an understanding of pathology. Such a stance implicitly conceptualizes the family as a system. One cannot read the major theorists of family therapy without a good knowledge of system theory and how it applies to the system we call the "family."

Block and La Perriere have observed " . . . that what unites family therapists is the intention to change the family system." Also that as a technique family therapy " . . . deals directly with a natural system . . ." and seeks to alter that system in some significant way.(1)

Satir, Jackson, Haley, and Bowen can all be classified as system theorists in that a general system approach underlies their thinking. The late Nathan Ackerman alone among major thinkers in the field would maintain that family therapy had not reached a sufficient level of development to warrant calling it a system approach to pathology. However, Ackerman would admit that the general system theory was the major theoretical concept in the field (as we learned in interviews at the Family Institute in New York, January 5th and 19th, 1971).

General system theory had as its prime mover the late Ludwig von Bertalanffy, a biologist. After many years of thought, he first presented it in 1945 and later showed how it might be applied specifically in the field of psychiatry.(2) Von Bertalanffy sought to find those principles which would be valid for all systems—for systems in general. He was concerned about wholeness and organization rather than reduction, "the nothing but approach" then prevalent in the field of science. General system theory has been called " . . . a new approach to the unity-of-science problem which sees organization rather than reduction as the unifying principle, and which therefore searches for general structural isomorphisms in systems."[2 (p 7)]

SYSTEMS

What are systems? In what do systems basically consist? Von Bertalanffy states that systems are "complexesof elements standing in interaction."(3) As such it is clear that system thinking is not limited to any single subject but applicable in many diverse ways.

The search for underlying patterns in reality itself is not a phenomenon restricted to von Bertalanffy's research. Many others, thinkers in a variety of fields, have been searching for the basic structures of reality, the patternings which are common to our experience. This search goes by the general name of structuralism and "connotes a belief that there is in all human social organization and behavior an underlying unifying structure or pattern."(4)

Levi-Strauss in anthropology, Noam Chomsky in linguistics, Jean Piaget in developmental psychology, in addition to von Bertalanffy are engaged in structuralism. It is, as Edgar Levenson has noted, of extreme importance because it is not just another way of viewing reality but a paradigm, a model which enables us to see a new pattern and, therefore, a new reality.[4 (pp 43–53)] To put it more simply: structuralism as seen in system theory gives us a new *gestalt.* The pieces of the picture are the same but the way in which they are seen is quite different. To view pathology from the point of view of a person and to see it from the point of view of a system is not just to get another picture but to see a new reality, a new picture.

To illustrate the differences in viewpoint, one might take a look at *The Glass Menagerie* by Tennessee Williams.(5) If one looks at Laura as a person apart from her family system (mother, brother), she appears to be a girl living in unreality and fantasy, at best, an ambulatory schizophrenic. She is "sick" and the labeled patient. However, if one looks at Laura from a system viewpoint as an element in a system in interaction, a very different picture is given. She is no longer the weak, sick, sister waiting for a "gentleman caller" but a person who performs a critical role in the family system. She is the one who maintains the balance or homeostasis of the system, without whom the system would collapse. One might say that whenever the tensions between Amanda and her son Tom get too high, Laura steps in to reestablish the system and to keep it going. The system functions precisely because of Laura's intervention and not in spite of it. One could say then that it is a false picture of reality to label Laura as "sick." More precisely, and more accurately, one should say that the Winfield family system itself is "sick," and Laura is only a symptom of that sick system.

The paradigm that a system approach gives is not the one that an intrapsychic paradigm gives. This is why issues which seem to be abstract and not germane to practice are in reality critical to how one proceeds. The treatment of the Winfield family will be quite different depending on a therapist's viewpoint. As we shall see both Don Jackson and Jay Haley, in particular, will elaborate on the importance of the paradigm for therapy.

PROPERTIES OF AN OPEN SYSTEM

Von Bertalanffy maintains that there are two kinds of system: an open system and a closed system.(6) The former, found in a family, is characterized by a continuous flow of component material, whereas the latter does not have such a continuous flow. Moreover, an open system has three properties: wholeness, relationship, and equifinality.

A system is not made up of independent parts but rather interdependent parts. Therefore, a system is not the total sum of its parts but is characterized to some extent by wholeness or unity. One is reminded of the geometrical axiom that the whole is greater than the sum of its parts. Again we must recall von Bertalnffy's definition of system that systems are "complexes of elements . . . in interaction." Without the interaction there is no system but merely adding up separate entities. The system of the family in *The Glass Menagerie* is not the sum of the individual personalities of Amanda, Laura, and Tom Wingfield but the vital, ongoing interaction between them. Von Bertalanffy uses the term *wholeness* to characterize such an interaction.

The second property which flows from this is *relationship*. If an entity, for example, the Jones family is not seen in isolation or cannot be seen as such, one cannot analyze the persons independently because this is to distort the picture. The only viable alternative to this is to study the connections between the parts and to see how they interact. The term relationship then in system theory has a technical meaning and refers to the basic structures of the elements and how they relate. Furthermore, in system theory these elements are isomorphs or transformations of each other.

Von Bertalanffy uses the color spectrum to illustrate the concept of transformation.[3 (p 241)] The color spectrum ranges from violet to red on a continuum. A person who is not color blind can be taught that green is opposite to red and in many societies is a signal of danger. Halfway between red and green we find yellow on the color spectrum. Thus, the green, yellow, red of the color spectrum and the go, warning, and stop of our traffic signals have the same structure and are isomorphs or transformations of each other.

On the perennial question of the relationship of content to form, the structuralist will insist that it is the latter which determines the former, so that what seems widely divergent is, in fact, similar (analogies) as well as transformations of each other (homologies).

Levenson suggests, following Levi-Strauss' anthropological thinking, that there is a pattern in eating as well as in traffic lights. The system of transformation is as follows: raw to boiled to roasted as against poverty, sustenance, and wealth; or eating alone, family dinner, and feeding the chief. With tongue in cheek, Levenson remarks that serving the cannibal chief boiled chicken would be as serious a *faux pas* as serving boiled chicken at a suburban Bar Mitzvah.[4 (pp 34–35)]

Beneath the apparent humor of such a social gaucherie, there is a profound insight into how human beings put their world together: content changes but not structure. This leads to the third property of system, namely, *equifinality*. This means that no matter where one begins, the conclusion will be the same. Von Bertalanffy calls this the reason why "the same final state may be reached from different initial conditions and in different ways."[3 (p 40)] A closed system does not have this property of equifinality since its final state is determined by the initial conditions.

This property of equifinality is not new in human thought. The medieval scholastics had an axiom: whatever is received is received according to the manner of the one receiving. Apparently, this axiom has great relevancy for the clinician. For example, if one takes a system view of an ongoing interrelationship such as a marriage, it is not necessary nor even useful to spend a long time getting a history of the couple. Whether the subject is money, sex, children, or in-laws, the pattern will be the same. Equifinality operates in any and all cases. The clinician need only get some idea of the couple's interaction in a given area to understand how they relate. The seemingly abstract concept of equifinality, then, has great practical consequences for the therapist.

FEEDBACK

There is a final question to answer. "If the elements of a system are not the sum of their parts, how are they related?" Von Bertalanffy answers by saying that they relate through a process of feedback which maintains the system's functioning. Feedback is not derived from a cause–effect model, that is, *a* affects *b* affects *c*, and so on, but from a cybernetic or circular model, *c* leads back to *a*.

Thus a system approach gives us a new model or paradigm, which, in turn, influences practice. In the old paradigm "sickness" meant some kind of breakdown of the machinery of a person. If one uses the classical Freudian divisions of id, ego, and superego, then pathology is conceptualized as a malfunctioning of the parts; for example, an obsessive-compulsive neurotic is characterized as having a punitive superego. His intrapsychic machinery has broken down. In the new paradigm, however, the malfunctioning of a person is not caused by this but to a failure of his system to function properly because of a lack of information. Treatment, therefore, consists in correcting the informational gap, that is, changing or altering the feedback mechanism.[4 (pp 54–75)]

Feedback can be either negative or positive. The former is that type which corrects a system which in trouble and reestablishes its previous state. Clinically, the role of the "identified patient" frequently illustrates negative feedback. When the relationship between mother and father, for example, becomes overly intense and appears to be threatening the family system with disintegration, the "identified patient," often the family scapegoat, will "act out." This enables mother and father to unite once again, to stay together "for the sake of the children," and to save the family system.

On the other hand, positive feedback is that which can destroy a system. It uses tactics which force the family into new ways of acting by making old positions untenable. It produces what Jackson calls "runaways" in a system. It uses paradoxes to accomplish its goals as in much of the work of Haley.

In all cases, however, it is not isolating this or that person and using the label "sick" or "identified client." It is looking at the ways in which the system operates and producing movement not through changes in intrapsychic forces but by the use of feedback which changes the pattern of how the system works. Again, we can see how the paradigm one chooses influences how one does therapy.

PARADIGMS

It is clear to the reader that paradigms are important. One sees what one wants to see. One frame of reference produces different material than another because it looks at different dimensions. Levenson has suggested that in therapy there have been three models: the work machine model, the communication model, and the organismic model.[4 (pp 68–70)] In the first model cure was a going back and an undoing of the past. In the second model cure is in the present, in the here and now. In the third model, the organismic, the emphasis is on organization, so that "we are no longer as interested in the machinery as we are in its *patterns of consequence.*"[4 (p 70)]

Family therapy from its inception has stressed the importance of communication within the family system. From the beginning it has used a communicational model. We have just briefly examined the seminal ideas that derive from this model. It is time now to look at those thinkers who have developed the most complete and significant body of work in the field of family therapy. This then will enable us to look into the future to see how family therapy is now moving toward the third model, the organismic.

Perhaps, we can best summarize this section on paradigms and their importance by once again quoting Levenson:

The communication theorists and family therapists are the first relatively pure second paradigm therapies. Family therapy, at its inception, focused on the failures of communication between members of the family. It has, more recently, shifted to an interest in the family as a perspectivistic whole and the family members as transformations of each other. In this sense, members of the family invent each other. Rather than communication, the focus is now on control and organization. Family therapy and group therapy (the artifactual family) have moved most easily into the third paradigm, of organismic relationships.[4 (p 67)]

NOTES AND REFERENCES

1. Block D, La Perriere K: Techniques of family therapy: A conceptual framework, in Block D (ed): Techniques of Family Psychotherapy A Primer. New York, Grune & Stratton, 1973, p 4

2. Gray W, Rizzo N: History and development of general system theory, in Gray W, Duhl F, Rizzo N (eds): General Systems Theory and Psychiatry, Boston, Little, Brown, 1969, pp 7–31

   This article gives a brief but adequate treatment of the subject. Part Three "General Systems Theory in Action," pp 311–467, is of special value as it shows at length how GST can be applied in family process.

3. Von Bertalanffy L: The meaning of general system theory, in General System Theory. New York, Braziller, 1968, p 33

4. Levenson E: The Fallacy of Understanding. New York, Basic Books, 1972, p 31

   Levenson is brilliant, well read, and writes with wit and humor about the impact of structuralism on psychoanalysis.

5. Williams, T: The Glass Menagerie, New York, New Directions, 1966

6. Von Bertalanffy L: General system theory and psychiatry, in Arieti S (ed): The American Handbook of Psychiatry, vol 3. New York, Basic Books, 1966, pp 702–721

Summary of Part I

We have entitled this part "Seminal Ideas in Family Therapy" because the five concepts studied have been the most important in the field and the most productive of further research.

In the 1950s, as Murray Bowen pointed out, various people began research independently with the notion that there might be some significant connection between the pathology of an identified schizophrenic patient and his family system.(1) During the decade from 1950 to 1960 this research began to unfold especially in Palo Alto, Bethesda, and New Haven in this country, and in Europe at the Tavistock Clinic in London.

The clinical hunch that there might be an important link between a labeled patient and his family system began to show results. Prior to this research, lacking any solid evidence, one could only speculate about its importance. From the time of Bleuler on, therapists had noted family interactions and speculated on their importance in the etiology of schizophrenia. Moreover, one could show statistically that persons who were labeled as schizophrenic tended to beget others with similar problems. But the links between the identified patient and his family system had not been made more precise. The process by which this took place, which one might call the transmission of irrationality, had not been well investigated.

In addition to the relationship between the patient and his family system, a second area of importance, known for a long time by clinicians, was the difficulty the identified client had in getting out of his family system. There was a relationship between the two that was hard to describe but which had something of the qualities of adhesive or gum, a stickiness that made moving out of the family almost impossible. Furthermore, the boundaries between the patient and the family tended to shift and move. They were not clearly marked or defined, stretching almost endlessly but never breaking and allowing a family member to leave. Moreover, the barriers between the generations were not maintained, and frequently there was an alliance between the schizophrenic and one of the parents which excluded the other parent.

Communication, too, was muffled and unclear. Messages were sent which could not easily be decoded. They seemed to say one thing at one level, and another thing at another level. The net result for the patient was confusion and his response to this was silent withdrawal. The levels of verbal and nonverbal communication did not match. The client was bewildered and mystified. He began to doubt his sanity and his ability to unravel messages. A pervasive kind of fear marked the personality. It was not safe for him to venture out beyond the family nest so he stayed close to home. Outsiders were looked on with suspicion, and the patient looked for guidance only from the family.

Wynne and Lidz began to examine these factors more closely through interview, observation, the use of Rorschach protocols, and other methods. Bateson, and the group from Palo Alto, formulated the communicational processes in terms of the double bind theory. Laing endlessly interviewed the families of his schizophrenic patients noting in particular the communicational patterns which were prevalent.

The outcome of this research was most productive. First of all, the clinical hunches regarding the schizophrenic and his family were for the most part confirmed. Second, and more importantly, the results were not confined only to the schizophrenic and his family but could be extrapolated to other family systems. The processes that were detected in severely disturbed families did not have to be restricted but could be applied more or less to so-called normal families. Finally, these investigations were fruitful and allowed for further research. They supplied the therapist with "handles" which enabled him to deal with family systems. At last, he had a terminology which could be used with distressed families.

The terms *double bind, pseudomutuality, schism* and *skew*, and *mystification* were created to describe multiple simultaneous phenomena. These terms were needed because the language of therapy then in vogue did not have a terminology adequate for the investigation. The paradigm used did not account for multiple interpersonal interactions. Obviously, a new paradigm brings new results.

The invention then of the new terminology resulted from the use of a new paradigm which we have called the communicational model. The general system theory, as articulated by von Bertalanffy, supplied the paradigm with its emphasis on feedback and information rather than on insight and cure. A new language implies a new paradigm. One cannot invent a new thing without at the same time inventing a new hypothesis. The old hypothesis gives the old results.

The seminal ideas of the early days of family therapy are the result of a structuralist approach. It is not important, one should note, that the people involved necessarily be conscious of what they are doing to produce results. Indeed some of them may be startled to know they are structuralists. This is of little import as Levenson wryly remarks that " . . . structuralism, like fornication, is practiced with considerable proficiency and gusto by people who would be surprised to learn its proper name."(2) The seminal ideas of family therapy are the result of a structuralist point of view.

To conclude this summary of Part I, it is appropriate to refer again to Ronald Laing's contribution. For him the paradigm is supreme. The model used is critical because it determines what is seen. I mentioned earlier Laing's debt to Sartre's existential thinking and yet in some ways his approach to therapy is more similar to Heidegger's(3) approach to philosophical truth. Both approach reality as a disclosure of the phenomenon observed. Heidegger uses the Greek work *aletheia*, an unmasking, to describe this process. Laing(4) similarly does not prove his point or give evidence, he presents a viewpoint or a frame of reference, which will unmask and present a new picture. It is a structuralist point of view using a paradigm that emphasizes patterns. It is a paradigm that is different from the work machine model of Freud and one that goes beyond the communicational model. It is a paradigm that points toward the future in which perspective and structure are the essential elements.

It is now time to examine in detail how these seminal ideas developed in the history of family therapy by seeing how they were used by the seminal theorists in the field.

NOTES AND REFERENCES

1. Bowen M: The use of family theory in clinical practice, in Haley J (ed): Changing Families. New York, Grune & Stratton, 1971, pp 159–192
2. Levenson E: The Fallacy of Understanding. New York, Basic Books, 1972, p 30

3.   Heidegger M: Being and Time. New York, Harper & Row, 1966
4.   Laing R: The Divided Self. Baltimore, Penguin, 1965

     Here Laing gives some good examples of his technique which we label as
     "uncovering."

PART II

Seminal Theorists
in Family Therapy

Introduction

In a work commissioned by the Group for the Advancement of Psychiatry on the family, *The Field of Family Therapy*,(1) the therapists in the survey listed Virginia Satir, Nathan Ackerman, Don Jackson, Jay Haley, and Murray Bowen as the most influential thinkers in the field. There is little doubt that the survey taken originally in 1967 would be changed, today. Certainly, Bowen's influence has grown since then, and he would be more highly placed, and perhaps Minuchin added, otherwise the list would remain unaltered. There are five seminal thinkers in family therapy.

To make what follows more understandable to the student, I present the basic concepts of each theorist and then propose three questions which should show how each theorist views a family, how change is produced in a family, and the role of the therapist in that change.(2)

What is the purpose of a family? How does a family function? What roles are assigned to the various members? What are the goals of a family? These are some of the major considerations which can be grouped under the heading of "What is a family?"

From this flows a second question: "What should the outcome of family therapy be?" Frequently, a family unit is experiencing difficulty in functioning and trys to correct itself. Often, at the suggestion of a school counselor, who tells a parent that the problem they are having with a son may not be solely a personal one but may involve the way the family functions, the parents turn to a family therapist. It is a decision they make perhaps reluctantly after much debate, pain, and embarrassment. What should happen in the encounter between the therapist and the family? Should the relationship between the parents be examined? If so, how much examination is needed? What about the siblings? To what extent should they share in the lives of their parents? What about family secrets?

It is clear that to some extent the outcome of family therapy should be one of change. But to what extent or degree? How is change measured in a family? Is relief of symptoms enough? Is family therapy really "deep therapy"; that is, does it get at the roots of pain and trouble and alleviate them or is it only a palliative measure? The outcome of family therapy is clearly a critical concern.

Finally, a third question must be asked: "What is the role of the therapist?" This is a "how" question. Once we know something of the way a theorist views a family, and what he thinks the encounter between himself and a family should produce, we then ask a further question of his role in the process of change. Is insight the goal of family therapy? If so, then is there an analogy between the role of the therapist in family therapy and that of the analytically oriented therapist? If insight is not a goal, is it symptom removal? Does the therapist reduce or diminish the pain in the family? How does he do this? Is he passive or active? Does he use transference, or not? Is it encouraged, or not? Is he a teacher or role model for the family? All these questions are important if we are to understand the nature of the therapeutic relationship between the therapist and the family.

After we see the basic concepts of our five major thinkers, we can then ask them our three basic questions. This will enable us to understand how the key thinkers in family therapy understand their therapeutic medium. It will allow us finally to look more minutely at a series of dimensions so that we get a precise idea of the similarities and differences between family therapists.

We begin our analysis with Nathan Ackerman for two reasons. First, Dr. Ackerman forms a bridge between the old and the new.(3) He stands midway between the intrapsychically oriented therapist(4) who is only peripherally concerned with families in so far as they throw light on the person who is seen as client, and those people who aptly are called system analysts because their concern is not the person but the way in which the system functions; that is, the system is the patient and not this or that person.

Dr. Ackerman sees family therapy as operating under a series of hypotheses which include elements of the intrapsychic, the interpersonal, and the system approach to therapy, as he stated in an interview at the Family Institute in New York on January 5, 1971. To put it more simply: he opted for a *both/and* position rather than an *either/or* position.

For him the bridge between the intrapsychic and the system concept is found in the notion of role relationships. This is so because the notion of role necessarily implies at least an interpersonal relationship. To talk about mother necessarily involves a child. To talk about the role of husband implies that of wife and vice versa. A role relationship concept means some kind of reciprocity. On the one hand, it goes beyond the intrapsychic to the interpersonal, and on the other hand, it does not deny the intrapsychic in the name of the system as Haley would, for example.(5)

Ackerman then tries to hold on to both ends of the spectrum, the intrapsychic and the system approach. These theoretical concepts may be more easily seen in a diagram (Fig. 1).

A second reason for beginning with Ackerman is an historical one. He was the creator of family therapy, the "grandfather" of the movement, who was a brilliant and articulate spokesman to a rather hostile psychoanalytically oriented medical community.(6) It is appropriate as well as necessary to begin with Dr. Ackerman's concepts to understand how it all began and how family therapy evolved.

Fig. 1.   Theoretical spectrum of family therapy.

Systems approach	Role relationships	Intrapsychic approach
←		→
eg, Jay Haley	eg, Nathan Ackerman	eg, Martin Grotjahn

NOTES AND REFERENCES

1. Group for the advancement of psychiatry. Field Fam Ther 7 (78):570, 1970
2. This suggestion was made by Dr. Homer Jernigan of Boston University
3. Meissner W: Thinking about the family-psychiatric aspects. Fam Process 3:1–40, 1954

   The author suggests that family therapists can be divided into three categories: intrapsychically oriented, role relationships, and system analysts.

4. Grotjahn M: Psychoanalysis and the Family Neurosis. New York, Norton, 1960

    Although the author is sympathetic to family process, basically he sees pathology as residing in the person. He opts for the medical model of sickness and health, whereas a system analyst would see pathology more in terms of the system. For further clarification see Part One "The History and Development of Psychoanalytic Family Therapy," pp 19–83

5. Haley J: Strategies of Psychotherapy. New York, Grune & Stratton, 1963, p 151

    Haley writes: " . . . psychopathology is a product of a power struggle between persons rather than between internal forces. This shift from conflict within to conflict without requires a major rethinking of psychiatric theory."

6. Framo J (ed): Family Interaction. New York, Springer, 1972

    Framo dedicates this book, a report of a conference held in 1967, to Dr. Ackerman under the title of "grandfather" of family therapy.

6

Nathan Ackerman

In 1938, Nathan Ackerman in writing about the family made the observation that it was a unit in itself, having its own psychological and social life.(1) In the same article he makes two other observations. One is that the family unit is not static but is dynamic and changes at different times because of internal and external pressures. The other is that the family is an exchange medium and the values exchanged are love and material goods.[1 (pp 55–56)] In a sense Ackerman's fundamental approach to therapy is contained in the notion that there is a constant interchange occurring between the person, his family, and society. To fully understand how a person functions, it is necessary to see him in all these aspects. They are not isolated components, they are in constant interaction, the one influencing the other.

Thirty years later, these concepts seem less striking than when first written. However, the shift in perception away from an almost exclusive orientation toward the intrapsychic to an interpersonal and especially to a family concept is mostly attributed to the writings of Ackerman. His task for over 30 years was to elaborate on the seminal notions just mentioned.

Ackerman stands as a bridge between the individual (intrapsychic) approach to pathology and the system approach, as seen in the communicational theorists. Trained as a psychiatrist and psychoanalyst, but also influenced by social psychology, Ackerman tried to combine both strains in his theorizing: "My personal synthesis of personality theory makes use of Freudian dynamics for understanding the internal mental processes but emphasizes the adaptational view of personality, man in society."(2) Ackerman's basic stance is that there is a continuing dialogue going on between heredity and environment. He would maintain that neither can be considered apart from the other.

The "either-or" approach (ie, either the biological processes or social forces are the main determinants of personality) is simply not tenable in the light of presentday evidence. It is a polemic which raises a false and irrelevant question, one for which there can be no scientific answer.[2 (p 48)]

However, Ackerman did not consider himself a system theorist since he felt such a concept was premature in the development of family therapy. In an interview on January 5, 1971, he said: "I would opt for a set of hypotheses rather than hold for a system at the present time." Nevertheless, he maintained: "Some kind of theory is necessary which includes two things: a theory of the family and a relationship between family theory and "mental illness."

SOCIAL ROLE

The key concept for Ackerman, among various hypotheses, is that of social role. "As a bridge between the processes of intrapsychic life and those of social participation, it is useful to employ the concept of social role."[2 (p 53)] Ackerman defines social role as " ... the adaptational unit of personality in action," and for practical purposes regards it as synonymous with the concept of "social self."(3) Ackerman sees social role as a semipermeable membrance in that it permits a limited penetration in both directions, that is, between the environment and the self. In general, Ackerman's thinking on social role has been influenced by Kurt Lewin. More specifically, as applied to therapy, it perhaps has been stated best by John Spiegel with whose thinking Ackerman was in general agreement as we discussed in one interview.

Thinking of the family in terms of roles has several advantages. First of all, it enables one to describe a more than two-person system or a plurality of transactions, as well. Second, roles are always complementary or reciprocal.

In actual practice Ackerman was always thinking in terms of roles. What does it mean to be a mother or father? How do you want your child to act in this instance? What are the expectations established in this family? Unless the roles are clearly delineated and more or less agreed on, the transactions within the family will not go smoothly.

Focusing on these areas of conflict enabled Ackerman to narrow down the complaints within the family and to help the people work on certain issues. It is a technique for getting at the specific problems that exist.(4)

Ackerman begins his book *Treating the Troubled Family* with a long excerpt from a family session. He then comments on what he has tried to do:

> He (the therapist) pierces the misunderstandings, confusions, and distortions, so as to reach a consensus with the partners as to what is really wrong. In working through the conflicts over differences, the frustrations and defeats, and the failure of complementarity, he shakes up the old, deviant patterns of alignment and makes way for new avenues of interaction.(5)

If there has been a "failure of complementarity," how does one go about making the role more complementary? As noted previously, Ackerman feels that John Spiegel has some relevant comments to make in this area. Spiegel lists five causes for the failure of complementarity: cognitive discrepancy (one does not know what is required), goal discrepancy, allocative discrepancy (eg, because of sex or age, one is a victim), instrumental discrepancy (eg, money), or discrepancy in value orientation.(6)

Furthermore, Spiegel suggests that by the use of role induction (ie, by changing another's concept of the role, eg, by coaxing, coercing, masking, evaluating, or postponing) or by role modification (ie, by a change in both parties, eg, by exploring, compromising, consolidating, or referral to a third party), a therapist can produce complementarity. If either of these proves unsatisfactory, a role reversal can be tried.

To watch Ackerman in action on video tapes is to see Spiegel's theorizing turned into practice. The concept of role then for Ackerman was an abstraction as well as an idea that gave birth to how one goes about doing family therapy. Also note that Ackerman is more inclined to deal openly with the question of a value system than some other family therapists. He sees this as tied in to the process of therapy itself, as woof and warp. He writes: "The basic question is: Does the problem of values belong to the question of psychotherapeutic cure, or doesn't it? I believe firmly that it does."[5 (p 49)]

This is another area in which Ackerman would part company with some of the communication theorists. He feels that clarity of communication and understanding the other is not enough. It is not just the process of communicating that is important but the content, as well. He feels this is, to a large extent, ignored by many in the field. He writes: "It (therapy) must be oriented not only toward the aim of freedom from but also toward the further aim of freedom for a set of positive goals in life."[5 (pp 56–57)]

One might make the observation that to work on roles or to seek a clarification of how people relate is a part of any kind of therapy and not exclusive to family therapy. However, what makes it different theoretically is that the roles are seen as part of a wider system of interaction. Ackerman, like all family therapists, ascribes to the concept of family balance or family homeostasis.[2 (pp 68–79)]

HOMEOSTASIS

Literally translated *homeostasis* means "staying the same." It refers to the capacity of restoring steady states following upsets of balance. However, as Ackerman uses it in his theory, it is a more dynamic and open concept. As he conceives it, homeostasis does not operate to restore a previous balance or level of functioning but is the principle which allows for change and growth within a given system:

I am suggesting that "homeostasis," or the principle of dynamic equilibri-um, signifies the capacity for creative, fluid adaptability to change, which at the same time assures that measure of coordinated control that prevents the organism from being overwhelmed by a barrage of stimuli in excess of the organism's capacity to accommodate (the final effect of which would, of course, be disorganization).[2 (p 70)]

Homeostasis, then, acts as the principle which allows for change within the system. It is not a principle for maintaining the "status quo" but for allowing a controlled "instability" or change within the system. This is why ultimately homeostasis is dynamic and not static. This brief explanation of homeostasis is sufficient for the present. We will discuss it again in our analysis of Jackson's thought.

The concept of homeostasis is a central one to family therapists of whatever school. Ackerman points out that homeostasis is not just limited to the family but applies to society, as well. He makes the point that the homeostasis of the person is dependent on that of the family, which, in turn, is contingent on that of the society. "These relations do not move in one direction only; they are, of course, circular and convoluted."[2 (p 74)]

With this notion we have come to the heart of Ackerman's theory. The chain of events that link the individual member to his family and to society, although able to be conceptualized separately, in reality, are interrelated. Therefore, pathology or illness at any one level necessarily means illness at all levels, since we are talking not about individual parts, but a totality.

Given this notion of the homeostatic balance within the family, one can easily see that pathology will be theoretically conceived as the unbalancing of the family homeostasis and not just of one person in it. This is why Ackerman will call the behavior of any one member of a family a " . . . symptomatic reflection of the emotional distortion of the whole family."(7)

Furthermore, Ackerman states there are three components of psychiatric illness: the intrapsychic, the interpersonal, and the psychosocial pattern of the family unit.(8) No one element can be looked at apart from its relationship to the others. Ackerman sees individual therapy related to family therapy as one part to another part, albeit a larger one.(9)

With the relationship of individual person to family and to society as background, we can now follow Ackerman's thinking as he tries to develop concepts which will explain three interrelated sets of processes:

1. What goes on within the person?
2. What goes on in between the person and other significant family members?
3. What goes on in the psychosocial patterns of the family as a whole?

Given his frame of reference, one can see how Ackerman has to conceptualize the family as an interactional unit, rather than as a system strictly speaking. In addition, the use of the concept of social roles makes much sense in forming hypothetical constructs about the various relationships at all three levels.

CORE CONCEPTS

Ackerman lists two core concepts by which the psychosocial dynamics of family life can be operationally defined. The first is psychological identity which subsumes strivings, expectations, and values. The second is stability of behavior, specifically in (1) continuity of identity in time, (2) control of conflict, and (3) adaptability and complementarity in new role relationships, that is, the capacity to grow and learn.[2 (p 82 ff)]

The concept of psychological identity is the answer to the question "Who are we?" that the family must ask. The concept is an attempt to explain why a given family is what it is. For Ackerman the question of identity of self and that of the family are inextricably woven. One depends on the other; one influences the other. Although they may be separated and examined apart from each other, diagnostically, this cannot be done. Ackerman writes: "The image of self and image of family are reciprocally interdependent. At each stage of development, personal identity is linked to and differentiated from the identity of parents and family in a special way."[2 (p 83)]

The second core concept is that of stability of behavior. It must be considered together with psychological identity. The sense of identity can only come about if there is a stability of behavior so that the two concepts are interrelated. Ackerman is saying that the family has to keep a sense of self in the midst of conflict, and yet, allow for growth and change. The old must be preserved but the new welcomed.

Again we are back to the importance of role relations in Ackerman's theoretical notions. Flexibility and adaptability of role is essential if the family's behavior is to be stable. Therefore, the role relations must allow for developmental stages in the life of the family, especially for the maturing autonomy of the children. When the family roles "fit," when the people are flexible, the behavior remains stable and a sense of shared identity is forged. When there is rigidity in the roles, or disagreement about the definition of them, there is difficulty.

Ackerman conceptualizes the interrelations of the family and the person in terms of identity and stability in the following diagram in Figure 2.[2 (p 87)]

Fig. 2.   Interrelation of Individual and Family

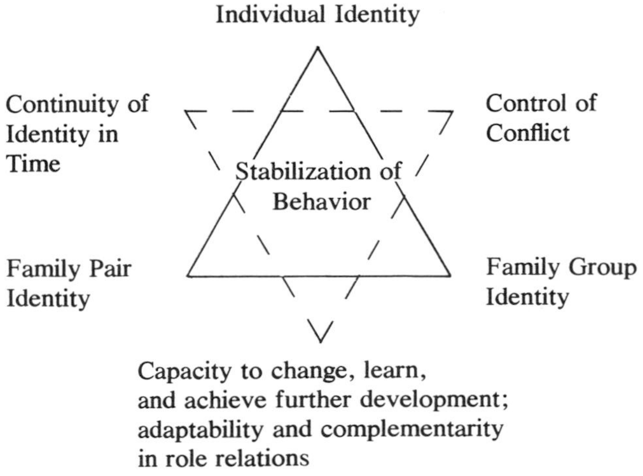

Individual Identity

Continuity of Identity in Time   Stabilization of Behavior   Control of Conflict

Family Pair Identity   Family Group Identity

Capacity to change, learn,
and achieve further development;
adaptability and complementarity
in role relations

PATHOLOGY

How then does Ackerman conceptualize the breakdown of healthy process within the family? It is not simply caused by the presence of conflict because this can be either catalytic or paralytic. It is attributed to a breakdown of role complementarity. The hallmarks of family unity are affection, caring, and loyalty and these are possible only through role complementarity.

In an attempt to correlate intrapersonal dynamics and interpersonal patterns, we must shift from an either/or position to a both/ and one position. To do this, to hold on to both ends of the process, Ackerman introduces the concept of role adaptation " ... which requires consideration of the phenomenon of the reciprocity or complementarity of role relations within the family group."[7 (p 89] Change, therefore, in itself, does not produce conflict. Change can mean growth or decline of either the person or the family depending on how well or how poorly it is handled. Growth, however, is dependent on

... the ability to accommodate to new experience, to cultivate new levels of complementarity in family role relationships, to find avenues for the solution of conflict, to build a favorable self-image, to buttress critical forms of defense against anxiety, and to provide support for further creative development."[5 (pp 90–91)]

In Ackerman's thinking, the constant adjustment to new roles is critical for both the person and the family. Social roles are thus the means of understanding the relationship between the person and the family. In Ackerman's colorful phrase, social role is the "semipermeable membrane" that permits an interaction between the environment and the self.[3 (7)] "When the balance of role relations and lines of communication is damaged, the family becomes emotionally split."[7 (p 48)]

Diagnosis then is a complex matter involving both the person and the family. This is a departure from the traditional approach which tends to see pathology as mainly intrapsychic. Ackerman strongly disagrees with this approach. "Clinical diagnosis is perforce only partial unless all these elements—individual, role, family group, and their interrelationships—are taken fully into account.[2 (p 109)]

CRITICAL ISSUES: NATHAN ACKERMAN

What Is a Family?

A family is a group with several purposes. One is biological: through the union of male and female to produce offspring and ensure their survival;(9) another is psychological and economic. The family is also an exchange medium, as noted previously, in which love and material things are exchanged. Finally, the family has a social purpose in that society needs the family to accomplish its goal so that " . . . society molds the function of family to its greatest usefulness."[2 (p 17)] "Basically, the family does two things: It ensures physical survival and builds the essential humaneness of man."[2 (p 18)]

In Ackerman's thinking the family is the key unit in society. The process of socialization, of making children into productive units of society, is the major task of the family. This process is carried out at two levels: the gradual task of weaning the child from dependence which is total (symbiotic) to that of independence and moving the child from a place of infantile omnipotence to a more realistically oriented view of self. The goal is to lead the child from the center of the family to a more peripheral position. The central role in this process, of course, is that of the parents, and yet at the same time, two other processes are going on.

First, the parents must join their separate identities into a union of themselves as a marital couple. Also, within this union each partner seeks further development as a person. What we have then is a combination of individual, marital, and family goals all interrelated. Ackerman therefore states:

Thus, the behavior of father, mother, or child cannot be evaluated in a social vacuum or in the exclusive context of parent-child interaction but must rather be regarded as a functional expression of the total interpersonal experience that characterizes the life of the family.[2 (p 22)]

What Should The Outcome of Family Therapy Be?

Ackerman writes that " . . . family therapy has a dual orientation: the dissolution of pathogenic conflict and fear, and the promotion of residual forces toward positive emotional health."[8 (p 164)] Ackerman sees family therapy as having two aspects: one eliminative, and the other additive. Therefore, he talks about phases of treatment in which one or the other will prevail. As is clear from the above statement, the therapist is very much in the role of teacher. It is also clear that values play an important part in the process of family change.

Ackerman states: "The goal of family therapy is not merely to remove symptoms or to adjust personality to environment, but more than that—to create a new way of living."[11] In the same book he further adds that it is not sufficient just to improve communications but that it is necessary to change attitudes as well.

In an interview (January 19, 1971) Ackerman said: "One of the goals of treatment is freeing up people to express emotion." As we have seen, he was concerned with the function of roles in the family. He theorized that people are either too rigid in their respective roles, and therefore are not open to new learning, or they are too fluid, and thus open to destruction of family life. The goal is to strike a balance between the two extremes. Healthy role adaptation lies somewhere between these two extremes. It is the optimal balance between continuity of the old and openness to new experience.

How Does a Family Change?

It changes when its conception of itself, its way of thinking, changes. If a family is having major problems, this usually requires outside help. The role of the therapist is to become a medium through which the change takes place. His first task is to get in touch with the feeling level of the family. The family has been infected with the "contagion" of doubt, despair, and hurt. The therapist must touch the family where it hurts and establish an empathetic rapport.

After doing this, the therapist then moves in and checks out a variety of family functions, such as its affectional relationships, the balance between dependency and autonomy, and the growth and development of each member in it. He gets at these issues by "tickling the defenses" of the family, that is, by a selective penetration of the defenses.[8 (p 162)] This enables him to locate the family problem and to shift the label of "sick" from the identified patient to the family. "The disturbance becomes recognized as a contagion of emotional pain with the whole family rather than the exclusive affliction of one member who is exploited to preserve a pathogenic family equilibrium."[4 (p 9)]

The therapist can then lead the family to a point where it begins to relate to each other in a different way. For example, the role of scapegoat would no longer belong to just one person so that the rest of the family would have to learn new and more appropriate roles. Note that the family chooses its own direction and that the therapist acts as a conductor not a composer. The therapist plays a number of different roles. Ackerman says that " . . . the family therapist must fit himself into a wide range of roles, as activator, challenger, supporter, confronter, interpreter, and reintegrator."[5 (p 101)]

How does a family change? It changes by shifting the balance within the family; by learning to relate to each other in new ways; and by examining its value system and deciding to make changes if that seems appropriate. The therapist is not the one who sets these standards or values for the family, but he assists in creating a new set of ways of acting and relating within the family. Therefore, the outcome of family therapy, ultimately, is not the responsibility of the therapist but the family.

At the beginning of our analysis of Dr. Ackerman's thinking, we noted that it was characterized by an interaction between the person, the family, and society. No doubt exposition of Ackerman's approach to family therapy has made this more obvious. For him to emphasize any one aspect at the expense of another would be a distortion. Such a conceptual framework sets him apart from many therapists who view themselves as system theorists and who consequently downplay the importance of the intrapsychic.

Dr. Ackerman, because of historical circumstance, came between an exclusively intrapsychic orientation and an emphasis on the system approach. He tried to show the former the future, and the latter the past. It was a difficult position to be in because one is often regarded by those with roots in the past as "radical," and by those with visions of the future as "conservative." Nevertheless, Dr. Ackerman is a family therapist who respected the contributions of those who proceeded him, at the same time, realizing that family therapy like any vital process must be open to change and the future. As such, he was truly the "grandfather" of family therapy in that he was old enough to appreciate the value of the past and its wisdom, but young enough to be aware of the importance of vision and the future. Because of these unique qualities he was a marvelous transition figure in the process of therapeutic change. It is unlikely that we shall again be blessed with one who was able to straddle two worlds and appreciate what both had to offer.

NOTES AND REFERENCES

1. Ackerman N: The Unity of the Family. Arch Pediatr 55:51, 1938
2. Ackerman N: The Psychodynamics of Family Life. New York, Basic Books, 1958, p 42
3. Ackerman N: Social Role and Total Personality. Am J Orthopsychiatry 21:1, 1951
4. Ackerman N: Family interviewing: The study process, in Ackerman N, Lieb J, Pearce J (eds): Family Therapy in, Transition. Boston, Little, Brown, 1970, pp 3–19

    Ackerman gives six brief cases of the techniques he uses in family therapy. Case number 3 especially illustrates the function of a distorted role in a family.
5. Ackerman N: Treating the Troubled Family. New York, Basic Books, 1966, p 39
6. Spiegel J: The Resolution of Role Conflict within the Family. Psychiatry 20:1–16, 1957
7. Ackerman N: Psychological dynamics of the "familial organism," in Galdston I (ed): The Family: A Focal Point in Health Education. New York, International Univ. Press, 1961, p 40
8. Ackerman N: Family focused therapy of schizophrenia, in Scher S, Davis H (eds): The Outpatient Treatment of Schizophrenia. New York, Grune & Stratton, 1960, p 165
9. Ackerman N: Interpersonal disturbances in the family: Some unresolved problems in psychotherapy. Psychiatry 17:367, 1954
10. Ackerman N: The Future of Family Psychotherapy, in Ackerman N, Beatman F, Sherman S (eds): Expanding Theory and Practice in Family Therapy. New York, Family Assoc. of America, 1967, p 4

7

Communication Theorists: Don Jackson, Jay Haley, Virginia Satir

INTRODUCTION

Our next three theorists, Don Jackson (Communication and Cognition), Jay Haley (Communication and Power), and Virginia Satir (Communication and Feeling), are considered together for a variety of reasons. First of all, at one time or another, they were all associated with the Mental Research Center in Palo Alto, California. More importantly, they shared a similarity of theoretical conception as well as a similarity of geographical location. They illustrate the model discussed at length in Chapter 5 under the notion of a second model paradigm. They do not conceptualize personality except in terms of interaction. The traditional model of the intrapsychic is simply not part of their theoretical framework.

A second reason for considering them together under the heading of communication theorists is that their main concern has been to improve the ways in which a family system communicates. This is a central concern. You may remember that both Jackson and Haley worked on the initial paper on the double bind and that each made a separate and significant contribution to it.(1) How messages are sent and how they are received in a family is a major concern for both. Satir, too, shares equally in her concern for the importance of communication in a family system. She writes: "If illness is seen to derive from inadequate methods of communication . . . it follows that therapy will be seen as an attempt to improve these methods."(2) The paths of communication then are not just part of a family system but an essential component of it for all three thinkers.

A third reason for considering them together is that they all share the common viewpoint that communication should not be limited to the verbal alone. Jackson will maintain that all behavior is communicative. Moreover, there is no opposite of behavior so that the idea of nonbehavior is contradictory. As Jackson says, one cannot not communicate.(3) Satir will agree with both Jackson and Haley on this dimension. Everything that happens in a family is communication and is significant. Communication is the common element which binds these three thinkers together. Nevertheless, they each emphasize different aspects of family interaction.

Jackson, as we shall see, was influenced by von Bertalanffy's approach to system theory. Therefore, one finds a heavy emphasis in Jackson on the cognitive aspects of communication so that what one thinks influences what one does. Thinking plays a major role in Jackson's approach to family therapy.

Haley has been influenced by hypnosis and especially by Milton Erickson's approach to it.(4) Haley sees the relationship between a therapist and his client as similar to that which occurs between a hypnotist and his subject. There is a power struggle between them. The question of who is in control of a relationship is critical for the outcome of therapy. Power and its meaning for therapy is a central concern for him. How one gains power and how one uses it is a central focus in the writings of Haley.

Finally, Satir is concerned about emotion or feeling in a family system. How one thinks, and who is in control are issues, and important ones, but how one feels toward himself and others in his system are the main concerns for her. Self-esteem and how it is acquired is the main issue for Satir. Feelings of acceptance or rejection are the focus in her therapy." "I think, therefore, I am" said the philosopher Descartes. "I feel moreover, I feel accepted," says the family therapist Satir.

Our study of communication theorists begins with Jackson because he wrote so extensively on the role of communication and was a cofounder with the late Nathan Ackerman of the magazine *Family Process*. In addition, it is very difficult to understand the ideas of Satir without first listening to Jackson since she accepts so much of his thinking as a basis for her practice. Next, I will present Haley who worked with Jackson initially and more recently has continued to influence the field of family therapy by pushing it beyond its original models and paradigms into new conceptual models. Finally, we will discuss Satir whose influence has been so great perhaps more because of her personality and effectiveness as a therapist than to her theoretical concepts.

DON JACKSON: COMMUNICATION AND COGNITION

The late Don Jackson, during his brief career, perhaps published more material on family therapy than any other theorist. Jackson constantly intertwined his clinical experience with theory to produce a rich but subtle conception of family process. In 1965, he stated that his basic theory rested on two clinically observable facts: first, the families of schizophrenics seemed almost deliberately to sabotage treatment of the ill member; second, when the ill member began to improve, frequently some other family member would fall ill.(5)

Jackson clearly was stating his observation that there is a balance within a family and that this balance constitutes an interacting system. Jackson would not deny the role of the intrapsychic but would feel that it would be inadequate to explain what happens in a family. A different model is needed. We have labelled this model a communicational model because the emphasis here is on communication.

Jackson would stress that although his emphasis on communication grew out of investigations with schizophrenics, it is not to be restricted to them alone. He would say that such a model was working in all family systems but at varying degrees of intensity. Jackson would view health or illness on a continuum and not see it as discontinuous. The key notion is more or less and not health or sickness.(6)

Homeostasis

The building block of Jackson's sytem is the notion of homeostatic balance which first occurred to him when he read one of Laforgue's early papers (1936) on schizophrenia. Jackson conceptualizes a family as a system which is maintained by an internal balance which he calls homeostatic. By this he means that the system operates within certain limits or parameters, which tend to remain fairly constant, and allow it to operate. Family homeostasis ". . . implies the relative constancy of the internal environment, a constancy, however, which is maintained by a continuous interplay of dynamic forces."(7)

Jackson translates this dynamic constancy into communication theory. He sees family interaction as " . . . a closed information system in which variations in output or behavior are fed back in order to correct the system's response."[7 (p 2)] Jackson spent the next 10 years refining this concept of communication and developing its implication. Fundamental to his thinking is the notion of a system:

> Initially, we can follow Hall and Fagen in defining a system as "a set of objects together with relationships between the objects and between their attributes in which *objects* are the components or parts of the system, attributes are the properties of the objects, and *relationships*" tie the system together.[3 (p 120)]

This description immediately frees Jackson from the intrapsychic because in this definition any object is specified by its attributes. Thus, if the objects in question are human beings, they are identified not by intrapsychic qualities but by communicative behaviors. Such "objects" then are best described not as persons but as persons communicating with other persons. The focus therefore is on the relationships within the system.

Jackson then offers his own definition of an interactional system: "two or more communicants in the process of, or at the level of, defining the nature of their relationship."[3 (p 121)] By this definition, Jackson has moved from a concept of health/sickness into a world of cybernetics and feedback. He has created a new way of looking at human interaction.

Jackson's thinking on systems has been widely influenced by von Bertalanffy's approach to it. You may recall that one of the properties of a system which he emphasized was that of equifinality which stated that the same final state may be reached from different initial conditions and in different ways. The importance of equifinality cannot be overemphasized when speaking of the family. As Jackson notes, it means that the genesis of a system is not as important as the organization of the interaction.

The Family: An Ongoing Interactional System

A system is stable with respect to certain of its variables if these variables tend to remain within defined limits.(8) Jackson accepts this description and conceptualizes certain properties of ongoing interactional systems. Such ongoing relationships are found in the family. In a family, however, unlike other groups, there is not just the now but a past and a future, a history. But Jackson is careful to avoid the analytic pitfall of asking why. He says it is sufficient to ask the question how do such relationships operate, and not to be concerned with the why. The focus then is not on the intrapsychic but the interpersonal.

Within an ongoing system there is a large variety of possible moves or changes but not an infinite one. There are limits within which one must operate. Communication in itself is a limiting factor since "every exchange of messages narrows down the number of possible next moves."[3 (p 131)] How this is so will become clearer when we talk about communication.

Communication is not only, nor even primarily, that of content but of how one person relates to another. The relationship is determined not so much by what is said as how it is said. The more sick the family, the more it fights over the definition of the relationship. The relationship tends to stabilize in the course of time and this stability has been labelled by Jackson as the rule of the relationship.(9)

As we noted earlier, wholeness refers to a change in any part of a system which means a change in the entire system. As applied to a family, Jackson notes:

> The behavior of every individual within the family is related to and dependent upon the behavior of all the others . . . Specifically, as noted above, changes for better or worse in the family member identified as the patient will usually have an effect on other family members . . .[3 (pp 134–135)]

The axiom of geometry, the whole is greater than its parts, states nonsummativity. A family, because it is an open, ongoing system, is not made up of the characteristics of the individual members, but by the interactional patterns which transcend the qualities of individual members. Because of this property, Jackson will approach family therapy with an eye on the interaction of the members of the system and not on isolated pathology. He demonstrates this in a long and brilliant analysis of the play "Who's Afraid of Virginia Woolf?"(10)

As the action between George and Martha, the protagonists, is analyzed, Jackson notes not that Martha is a sadist or that George a masochist, or vice versa, but how the dyad interrelates. This allows him to make statements about the interaction and avoid the use of clinical labels. It also gives us a clear demonstration of how the use of a system approach presents a picture very different from the one given an intrapsychic model of how George and Martha would relate.[3 (pp 149–186)]

The usual way of seeing interaction, that is, cause and effect, is bypassed. We can describe a four-person system by saying *a* affects *b* who affects *d* who affects *a* who affects *c*, to infinity. Linearity is ruled out and circularity introduced.

Theorists generally think that the balance or homeostasis is maintained by negative feedback. This kind of feedback keeps the balance or equilibrium at an operating level. The concept of rule holds that a system operates within certain limits. As applied to a family system, Jackson speaks of calibration as "constancy within a defined range."[3 (p 147)]

Calibration is a setting of the system akin to the use of the thermostat in a furnace. It allows the system to operate and controls its range or function. *Step-function* is a change in calibration. Step-functions have a stabilizing effect as they recalibrate the system and make it more adaptive. A family system, for Jackson, is characterized by wholeness, nonsummativity, homeostatis, and calibration.

Relationships are the fundamental building blocks of a family. All theorists, of whatever persuasion, would readily agree to this. However, Jackson conceptualizes these relationships not as entities in themselves such as mother and father, but more like particles in motion, and therefore, constantly changing. The way in which these relationships can be changed is the task of the therapist. But to change them he must first understand how they are established. This process of articulating a relationship is Jackson's core concept. It is done through communication. A relationship then is established by one person, a sender, transmitting a message (communication) to another, a receiver. However, instead of looking at either the sender or receiver abstractly, Jackson feels that the key to understanding is the nexus of the two. Therefore, the communication patterns give us not only information or content but how two or more people relate or process. The focus then is not the sender-sign or receiver-sign relations but on the sender-receiver relation as mediated by communication. This subtlety is the heart of Jackson's system theory, and the reason we label it a communication system theory.

Jackson makes the observation that behavior is a communication since it says something about how I relate. In addition, behavior, unlike most other qualities of life, does not have a negative. There is no such thing as nonbehavior; all behavior has meaning. The why of behavior has engrossed therapists, and in Jackson's view, unfortunately so. He feels, on the contrary, that to concentrate on the why is to miss the gold mine of interaction. For example, I may be angry at you because of some unresolved anxieties toward my father, or because of some other latent cause, but to center on this alone is to miss the way in which I relate to you. If we are bound together in a system, like a family, to miss this is to misunderstand how the system operates. Jackson has developed his thinking about communication into a series of axioms based on those properties that have fundamental interpersonal implications.[3 (pp 48–71)]

Axioms of Communication

Axiom 1.   The impossibility of not communicating. As obvious as it may seem, this axiom is often overlooked. Even silence or withdrawal is a communication and says something about a given relationship.

Axiom 2.   Any communication implies a commitment and thereby defines a relationship. This notion is borrowed from Bateson who calls these the report and command aspects of communication. The former is synonymous with the content, and the latter with the relationship. The relationship aspect of a communication classifies the content and is called a *metacommunication.* A metacommunication can be defined as "a communication about a communication."

These conceptual notions can be illustrated by an example. Saying either "Would you please open the window?" or "open that window" has about the same message content but shows a very different relationship. The former indicates a relationship of peers, and the latter one of a superior-inferior kind. The relationship aspect is usually not the one we are aware of, and in a healthy relationship it tends to be in the background. Persons with problems, on the other hand, tend to struggle constantly about the nature of the relationship.

Axiom 3.   The nature of a relationship is contingent on the punctuation of the sequence. Usually, we think of a sequence of exchanges as a stimulus-response pattern. Jackson suggests that this is not the way communication is viewed in a system concept. The pattern is a circular one rather than one of cause and effect. It is evident that many families quarrel endlessly over this issue of punctuation. Jackson notes that this yes-no-yes-no pattern of oscillation can go on to infinity and usually does.

Axiom 4.   Human beings communicate both verbally (digitally) and nonverbally (analogically). The former renders conceptual knowledge adequately but is poor in the field of relationship. The latter tells us more about a relationship but is unclear about the nature of the relationship. Apparently the nature of analogic messages is ambiguous. For example, tears can be of sorrow or joy, a smile a sign of acceptance or contemptuous rejection.

This axiom leads us to the conclusion that there must be an ongoing translation from one mode to the other. The simple question "What are you saying?" is, on analysis, a much more complicated one.

We are asking not only for the meaning of the concept but for what it says about a particular relationship. The analogic (nonverbal) becomes extremely important in family therapy precisely because the system is studied in interaction.

Axiom 5. All communicational exchanges are either symmetrical or complementary based on the kind of relationship that exists. If it is one of equality, that is, either party is free to take the lead, it is called *symmetrical*; if one leads and the other follows, it is called *complementary.* Of themselves they are merely descriptive terms and do not imply a value judgment. They can become pathological, however, when they get out of control. For example, when a symmetrical relationship continually escalates and leads to destruction or a complementary one hardens into petrification.

An Example of the Model

We can see how Jackson views the family as an ongoing, open, interactional system, and how his axioms of communication operate in a concrete way by again looking at the play "Who's Afraid of Virginia Woolf?" What is it that George does that sets off Martha and vice versa? What are the ongoing interactional patterns? The why fades into the background as we look for the how.

Jackson speaks of the "black box concept,"[3 (pp 43–44)] which allows us to see the importance of the how. The concept is borrowed from electronics. Electronic equipment had become so sophisticated that it was difficult to comprehend the internal workings of a device. As a result one concentrated on the input-output relations of the system without worrying about what went on inside. As the concept is applied here, it means that one does not have to talk about intrapsychic hypotheses but can look at the input-output relations in the system, that is, how Martha and George communicate. The therapist in Jackson's view can bypass the intrapsychic.

The interaction between George and Martha is not adequately described by "He does this and she does that, because of, and so on." More correctly, the process is a circular one in which "He does this in response to her, in response to him, and so on." Moreover, the because part is omitted. The therapist then does not get caught in the endless spiral of George and Martha. He observes the pattern and moves quickly to alter it. He punctuates the sequence differently which is why he can be effective.

If one looks at the communication that takes place between

George and Martha in the play, one gets a vastly complex view of their relationship. Again, the question of paradigm is significant and critical. If a reader focuses on one person and ignores the system, then the other person is merely peripheral. For example, to look at Martha from an intrapsychic point of view is to see an aging, articulate woman who is frustrated by her inability to achieve the social level she seeks. It is to see her unable to deal with her father, to have an unresolved oedipal complex, and one who projects on to her husband George her own intrapsychic problems. In such a view George is only peripheral.

Likewise, if one views George from an intrapsychic viewpoint, Martha fades into the background. George is a man unable to deal with his guilt. We are told that he is responsible for the death of both his parents, a fact he cannot forget, and one Martha will not allow him to forget. Apparently, it is this guilt complex which keeps him from attaining the academic success he seemed destined for originally. Martha exacerbates the problem but she is not the cause of it. She, too, is peripheral to his problem as he is to her's. Martha is "hung up" on her father; George is "hung up" on his guilt. Perhaps. This is the view one gets using an intrapsychic model.

However, if we shift to a communicational model, the picture changes and so do the questions. We are no longer delving into the past, into what happened, and into the why, but we shift into the here and now, into the present, and into the how, that is, the way the George-Martha dyad is currently operating.

In the traditional model, basically an intrapsychic one, the therapist was a pawn between the marital couple. He was equipped with medieval armor in the age of the jet. His tools were designed for a patient, and the reality he was meeting was interpersonal. As long as he was using the older model causality was always cause-effect. This meant he had to move from one side to another by favoring one or the other. Instead of breaking the existing pattern he only prolonged it until exhausted, and frequently angered by exorbitant fees, the couple declared a truce. Nothing was changed and hostilities would resume again.

In a communicational model, however, the therapist does not have to move from one to another. George will say the problem is A-B, A-B and Martha will say it is C-D, C-D. This will go on endlessly. But the therapist will say it is E-F, E-F. He will see the interaction in a different way. He will not get caught in their game and will allow them the possibility of changing their pattern. The why of the game becomes relatively unimportant and the how of it takes center stage.

I have labelled the section on Jackson "Communication and Cogni tion" because observing the interactional patterns seems to be his major goal. His emphasis is more on the head than the heart. Satir also looks at communication but her stress is on the kinds of feelings that get communicated in a family system. On the other hand, Jackson is less interested in how one feels and more concerned with the ongoing, interactional patterns which characterize what is called the family system.

CRITICAL ISSUES: DON JACKSON

What Is a Family?

Unfortunately, Jackson died in January 1968 before he could be interviewed. Fortunately, however, he left enough material so that we can reconstruct his answers to the key issues in family therapy. In addition to *The Mirages of Marriage* (11), there is a long interview in *Techniques of Family Therapy* (12) containing ample material.

"The family is an interacting communications network in which every member from the day-old baby to the 70-year-old grandfather influences the nature of the entire system and in turn is influenced by it."[11 (p 14)] In this sentence Jackson is putting together the two basic concepts of his thinking: communication and homeostasis. He is illustrating his axiom that $1 + 1 = 3$, or the whole is more than the sum of its parts. The family gets its start by marriage which itself is a complex unity. There are the system of the male, the system of the female, and the marital system derived from the interaction of the male and female systems.

There are three factors which operate in the initial stages of the family system. First, there is a determination regarding goals. Some are conscious and explicit; others, more implicit and not expressly articulated, for example, status or approval; and finally, unconscious goals. Each person brings to the marriage his goals and the marital system must evolve into a joint system of goals. The results of the merger are unpredictable. They can cause constant fighting or " . . . are capable of humanizing the most hopeless egoist."[11 (p 174)]

The second factor is the choice of mate. The kind of mate selected will limit the goals the family will have. Age, location of residence, education, health, and contacts with extended families are just some of the important things to be considered in the kind of mate chosen and its effect on subsequent goals.

The third factor is the initial type of family structure. "When people marry, the first important action which takes place is the attempt of each spouse to determine the nature of the relationship. . . ."[11 (p 92)] More simply, this means that each wants to achieve his or her own goals without making accommodations to the other. This accounts for much of the friction in the early stages of the marriage.

When a child is born, a new factor is added to the system, and the homeostatic balance is disturbed. This is why birth is always a crisis situation since it necessarily means a change in the family system. If a second child is born into the family, a new subsystem is created, namely, the sibling system. Therefore, in a family with two children, Jackson would say that the family system consists of the marital dyad, the parent-child relationship, and the sibling system. Yet, and this is the key point, it is not just the sum of these that makes the family but their interaction.

To determine what is going on in the family system, one has to look at the causes for the unbalancing of the homeostasis. What are the factors that are causing the family to feel pain and to seek help? To find out, Jackson suggests his second major concept: one must check out the lines of communication. What is being *said* and what is being *heard.* Specifically, have the rules of the system, often unconscious, been violated, and if so, in what way? Frequently, the *quid pro quo*, that is, the agreements among the members is disturbed. "When the *quid pro quo* ground rules are violated . . . trouble begins."[11 (p 181)]

What Should the Outcome of Family Therapy Be?

One result of family therapy should be to make clear the rules that operate in the family. If these can be outlined clearly, then the members of the family can do something about changing them. We can see how this can be accomplished in the initial session Jackson has with the Starbuck family. He examines such issues as what the family expectations are for the father, what the role of the daughter Sue is, and the family myth that mother is well despite her frequent trips to the hospital for mainly psychosomatic complaints. Jackson tries to open up these areas for discussion and hopefully for change.

The rules have been set up initially by the husband and wife and are passed on to the children. Jackson comments that after the marriage has been operating for a while, " . . . the *quid pro quo* pattern becomes an unwritten (usually not consciously recognized) set of ground rules."[11 (p 179)] The key issue then has to do with the making of family rules. Who has the right to do what to whom and when is a central issue. How these things get worked out normally occurs through the *quid pro quo*, in which things are negotiated, and the family tasks divided. Jackson observes: "To survive a system requires mutual responsibility, reward, security, and dignity."[11 (p 17)] When these requirements are not fulfilled the system experiences pain and if it cannot right itself by its own compensatory mechanisms, it will need outside help. This brings us logically to the third issue.

How Does a Family Change?

The family changes when it reaches a point of realizing it cannot establish a proper balance and seeks help. In the hands of a skilled therapist a new balance may be found. Jackson suggests specific areas to be followed in doing family therapy. The central question is the family homeostasis or balance. Jackson writes " . . . I think that in general I do watch for clues to family homeostasis. I don't pay so much attention to the content as to the kind of a shift that doesn't seem to fit."[12 (p 207)] Jackson looks for the inconsistencies in the interaction because these give him clues to the family homeostasis.

Knowing this the therapist can then disturb the system. "You don't really point it (the system) out, you disturb it first."[12 (p 201)] Jackson argues that it is necessary to upset the system in order that the members will see it as it really is. He says, " . . . A will always say, 'Well, I think it's A-X, B-Y,' and B will always say, 'No, it's B-Y, A-X.'" You can upset the system by saying, 'Well, I think it's C-Q' so that both of them are confounded."[12 (p 201)]

Such a technique, favored also by Haley and Satir, is called *relabeling*. It consists in picking up the other side of a statement, that is, " . . . simply taking the motivation that has been labeled in a negative way and labeling it in a positive way. . . ."[12 (p 200)]

Another favored technique is prescribing the symptom. This means telling a person to keep acting in the same way he has been. For example, in the Starbuck family, telling the parents to treat the daughter in the way they have been so that they might discover how they have really been treating her. This technique produces a "runaway" in the system. Jackson observes: "Prescribing the symptom is more likely to produce insight than telling people how the mind works."[12 (p 227)] With the help of the therapist the family begins to see itself in a new way. The system can then change the homeostatic balance, and find a new way of relating that is less painful and more goal satisfying.

Jackson's approach to therapy can be summarized by pointing out the four major areas of emphasis distinct to family therapy:

1. The therapist is not a passive listener but a participant observer who is most active in the therapeutic process.
2. A major goal is to change behavior rather than aiming at insight.
3. A focus on the here and now rather than delving into the past.
4. A concentration on the interaction of the system rather than the intrapersonal.(13)

In his brief but brilliant career, Jackson made significant contributions to the field of family therapy. Most notable is his work on the "double bind" and the refining of the concept of homeostatic balance in the family. Both of these are major ideas in the thinking of the communication theorists. It is now time to look at how two other theorists, Haley and Satir, use communication theory.

JAY HALEY: COMMUNICATION AND POWER

If one were to characterize the thinking of Haley, it might be best put under the title "The Power Tactics of Jay Haley." Haley is interested, almost exclusively, in the power struggle that goes on in a relationship between people and the maneuvers they use in the struggle. "Power tactics are those maneuvers a person uses to give himself influence and control over his social world and so make the world more predictable."(14)

There are two central ideas in Haley's thinking: a relationship takes place through communication and communication exists at different levels of meaning. In these he is in agreement with Jackson, but his emphasis will be different, stressing the power element in a relation. By a relationship, he means the way in which two or more people interrelate. In Haley's view, like Jackson's, this can be either one of equality (symmetrical) or inequality, in which one gives and the other receives (complementary). In the former case, the relationship is a competitive one. In the latter, it is the kind found in a superior-inferior one. Haley would insist that any relationship by definition is a power struggle and the people involved are constantly struggling to define or redefine the relationship.

Levels of Communication

Given this basic viewpoint, one can see that in a relationship the interaction is not linear but circular. A is not the cause of Bs behavior, but A may be responding to B who, in turn, has responded to A, and so on. Haley writes: "The ultimate description of relationships will be in terms of patterns of communication in a theory of circular systems."(15) The manner or way in which people respond to each other establishes the rules for behavior between them.

Therefore, what is important is not just what is said but how it is said. This is what Haley means by levels of communication. In addition to the first level, one of content, there is a second level, one which qualifies what is said on the first level. This level he calls _metacommunication._ For example, tone of voice, inflection, body language, intensity, all exist at this second level of communication. Moreover, Haley would insist that one cannot understand what is being communicated unless and until he knows both levels. Since people do not just communicate ideas abstractly but do so through the medium of themselves, they are always saying something about how they relate to others.

When the two levels of communication jibe, there is a complete unit of transaction. A message has been sent and received in a congruent way. However, when the two levels do not match, the communication is not clear and double messages are received. Haley illustrates this by citing a mother who said to her child: "Come and sit on my lap." However, he observes she did so " . . . in a way that indicated she didn't always want him to be so obedient."(16)

At one level, that of content, the mother was making a request of her child. Yet what was communicated, that is, what was received by the child, was a different message. The child picked up her metacommunication at another level, at the level of qualification, which was not congruent with a seemingly loving request. Haley would maintain that such a pattern is typical of the kind found in schizophrenic communication and, in fact, is one of the necessary ingredients in the development of schizophrenia. Such a confusion of messages at various levels raises the anxiety level. Does she love me, or not? Such questions arise from crossed lines of communication.

Defining the Relationship

The second step in the process of communication is the defining of the relationship. "When one person communicates a message to another, he is maneuvering to define the relationship."(17) This is the core notion in Haley's thinking. For here is the heart of the power struggle, the control of the relationship. In any relationship there are two problem areas: (1) What messages or what kinds of behavior are to take place; and (2) Who is to control what takes place.

In communication theory all messages " . . . are not only reports but they also influence or command."[15 (p 10)] The manner in which these reports get said asks for or requests some kind of response from the other person. Again, an illustration will clarify this.

A young man puts his arm around his girl friend. He does so in a congruent way, that is, with a tenderness which indicates he wants her to move closer to him. She now must respond in one of three ways. Either she will move closer (comply), take his arm away (reject), or leave it there but comment that she is allowing him to keep his arm there (qualification). This last option is one which allows the girl to control the relationship by saying that her boy friend operates but only with her permission. This example shows how the two problems cited above are always operative in a relationship. The kinds or types of behavior exchanged are part of the ongoing power struggle, and the ongoing attempt to define or redefine the relationship.

Elements of Communication

Haley further analyzes communication into four basic elements:

1. I
2. am saying something
3. to you
4. in this situation.[15 (p 89)]

The only way to avoid a relationship is to deny one of these four elements. This is precisely what the so-called schizophrenic does. In normal situations, the messages sent demand some kind of response, or comment. In communication, it is not content alone, nor even primarily what is exchanged, but the *way* in which people will relate. Haley would hold that the schizophrenic cannot discriminate levels of messages and therefore cannot communicate.

In Haley's conception then the role of the therapist is not just to help people communicate in the obvious sense of exchanging information but to help them realize that they are engaged in a power struggle in the relationship. The same power struggle goes on in any kind of therapy. Haley sees no real difference among the injunctions of the directive therapist, the Rogerian, or the psychoanalyst.[14 (pp 11–15)] Obviously, the techniques are different but the goals are not. Each kind of therapist controls the relationship but in a different way. By selecting the type of material reported, and commenting in his own way, the therapist controls the relationship.

With these ideas as background, we can understand Haley's

approach to family therapy. First, it is clear that pathology in the family will not be viewed as belonging to this or that member but to the system. Second, there will be a constant struggle for power and control in the family. Third, the role of the therapist will be different in that the therapist will relate to the family in his own way. Also he will intervene when he chooses to and not when the family requests. We will examine each of these in order.

First, the system and not the person is pathological. Underlying this idea are two premises: the identified client is only a scapegoat for the family; and as this person improves, other members suffer various kinds of distress and exhibit symptomatic behavior. Haley would go so far as to say that

The primary responsibility of the schizophrenic is to hold the family together. Although social scientists, even family therapists, have not yet the vaguest idea how to prevent a family from disintegrating, the schizophrenic child accomplishes this with ease.[14 (p 126)]

Although this type of behavior is more noticeable in schizophrenic families, it is not restricted to them, but is found clinically in most distressed families.

Second, there will be a constant struggle for control in the family. However, pathology will be seen as interpersonal rather than as intrapsychic. Haley would insist that the social forces about him mold a person and make him what he is. They are not incidental to him but essential. Haley writes " . . . psychopathology is a product of a power struggle between persons rather than between internal forces. This shift from conflict within to conflict without requires a major rethinking of psychiatric theory."[15 (p 156)]

This is an important point because Haley does not see a continuity between the individual and the family. Haley would hold quite the opposite, that is, external problems induce internal ones which only reflect them. Haley would insist that this communicative power approach is not just "an adjunct to previous ways of looking at human beings" but a "discontinuous change."[15 (p 152)]

With this must come a new way of looking at persons. The old ways of thinking are no longer valid once we accept a system approach. Haley then would differ from some other theorists, for example, Ackerman, in that he would insist on an either/or approach, whereas others would still hold for a both/and.

Third, the role of the therapist. The therapist is the agent who produces a family change. In all therapy there is a threefold process:

1.   Change is possible.

2. The patient must participate in bringing about the desired change.
3. The patient must look for and notice change.(18)

How does the family therapist induce change in the family system? First, the therapist offers the family " ... an educational factor to help them behave differently and therapeutic paradoxes to force them to do so."[15 (p 165 ff)]

The educational factor means the therapist as a model. Instead of telling the family how to act, he demonstrates by his interaction with them how one ought to act. Instead of entering one or another of the family coalitions, he moves in and out, taking sides, but never remaining allied with one faction against another. Again by insisting that the problem in the family is not just the identified client, but the system itself, he is forcing the family to think in a new way. In addition, he does not let himself get provoked, as so many members of the family do, but by responding on his terms, he controls the relationship. Finally, he is alert to the metacommunicative level and points this out to the family.

However, it is not enough for the therapist to be an educator. He must do a second thing, namely, become " ... a metagovernor of the system."[15 (p 174)] Haley sees three major tactics as useful in producing the desired change.

First, directives to the family which are ambiguous. For example, telling the family to express their real feelings. This cannot be ignored because even to refuse to talk about their feelings is to reveal them.

A second tactic is the emphasis on the positive. This involves a constant effort to relabel behavior. Haley cites the case of a man who went after his wife with an axe. The therapist's comment on this behavior was that it was the man's attempt to bring about a closer relationship with his wife!

A third tactic is the encouraging of usual behavior. In this case resistance to the advice can only result in change. For instance, asking a domineering woman to take charge of the family will often highlight her interaction and result in her wanting to recede more into the background.

What is important in Haley's approach is the question of control. If the therapist tells the domineering woman to lead, she is no longer leading but following the instructions of the therapist. In any case, the therapist is careful that he keeps control of the relationship.

This last point, the use of paradox, is specifically a contribution of Haley. He maintains that all therapies regardless of theoretical differences deal in paradox. In therapy, a situation is created in which

1. The therapist sets up a benevolent framework in which change is to take place.
2. He permits or allows the client to continue with unchanged behavior.
3. He provides an ordeal which will continue as long as the behavior remains unchanged.[15 (p 181)]

Like the Zen Master the therapist induces change in the client by the use of paradox.

Therapy is a power struggle in which the therapist must be in control if change is produced. Another factor in Haley's approach which is different is the role of awareness. It is not necessary for the family to become aware of their behavior for effective change to take place. This, too, is a departure from the traditional viewpoint of therapists.

Insight, awareness, or knowledge of how the system operates are all unnecessary. What produces change is the therapist's intervention into the family system. The why of change is not important because only the fact of change matters. This is consistent with Haley's view of therapy as a power struggle. In a power struggle what counts is the outcome, that is, who won the battle. The manner of victory, the strategy, is of secondary importance usually more of interest to the devotee than to the bettor. Likewise, in therapy the client is more interested in the outcome and the therapist more in the strategy that produces the change.

HYPNOSIS—A THERAPEUTIC MODEL

With such a framework one sees easily why Haley is so attracted to hypnosis as a model. In hypnosis, the subject wishes to be rid of some problem. The strategy of the hypnotist is not important to him but only the cure. This is beautifully illustrated in a case of a bedwetting couple reported by Milton Erickson.(19) By the use of indirect hypnosis, Erickson gets the couple to take over direction of their own lives and to cure themselves. The key to this, however, was Erickson's insistence that " . . . the absolute requisite for therapeutic benefits would lie in their unquestioning and unfailing obedience to the instructions given to them."[19 (p 66)] This for Haley is the heart of the matter, namely, who is in control of the relationship. In Erickson's approach the power struggle is in the open. He announces he is in control from the beginning, but as one reads the account of the case the question arises, "Is he really in control or not?" The use of paradox is evident.

Erickson had commanded the bedwetting couple deliberately to wet the bed before getting into it each night for a period of 2 weeks. At the end of this time they would be given 1 night off and could sleep in a dry bed on Sunday night. Erickson's continues, "On Monday morning, the 18th, you will arise, throw back the covers, look at the bed. *Only as you see a wet bed, then and only then,* will you realize that there will be before you another 3 weeks of kneeling and wetting the bed."[19 (p 66)] A final admonition was given that there would be no discussion or debate but only silence and obedience.

The outcome was that each night the couple, with considerable distress, wet the bed. However, on Monday the 18th when they awoke, the bed was dry! They started to speak but remembered the order to be silent. That night without speaking they "sneaked" into a dry bed and did so for the next 3 weeks.

Did the couple make the decision to change their behavior or did they follow the injunctions of the therapist? Did their unconscious perhaps obey the therapist? Did they realize the use of paradox? Is it really important for them to know the answer to these questions? Haley would argue that it is neither important nor necessary since change could be and in fact was produced without their understanding.

The use of paradox and illustrations of therapeutic power struggles abound in Haley's analysis of Erickson in *Uncommon Therapy.*(4) Haley calls this approach to therapy strategic because the clinician is in charge and determines how the therapy will proceed. There is to be sure an interchange between therapist and client but the outcome and direction must be chosen by the former. To focus on why people behave in a given way is useless and burdensome, and Haley suggests that interpretation, the "why" of behavior is precisely the reason people do not change. It is a carry over from the Freudian tradition of the nineteenth century. The intrapsychic then is one way of conceptualizing human behavior, but in Haley's mind it is not the only way nor the most effective way.

Family Stages

During the early stages of the family therapy movement, research focused on types of families. There was the hope that some kind of typology would be developed which would allow the clinician to classify families according to types. Just as one would speak about neurotics, character disorders, and psychotics based on certain symptomatology so also families based on certain interactional patterns could be classified. This hope has given way to another concept based on stages of development in the family. (This concept will be seen again in Murray Bowen.)

Beginning with courtship and proceeding to the disintegration of a family system with death, a family passes through a series of stages or crises. The fantasy of the engagement period yields to the reality of daily life. The birth of a child changes a dyadic system into a triad, and presents the possibility of alliances and splits in the family. The departure of the last child for school brings about a definitive shift into middle age for a couple. The marriage of a child brings still another period of adjustment and initiates the process of a return to the former dyadic state. All these situations can be described as normal or developmental. And all of them can cause problems in a marriage if one or another cannot make a transition.

What seems to happen in disturbed families is that several factors cluster at the same time. A combination of events produce symptomatic behavior in one or more members of a given family. A stage of family process together with some kind of disturbance and an external intervention combine to produce difficulty. Haley suggests that adolescent schizophrenia, for example, can be the result of a combination of a stage of family life when a child should disengage from the parents, together with some outside disturbance, coalesce so that the separation process is thwarted and bizarre behavior is produced.(21)

This notion takes us a step beyond the concept of certain types of family being "sick" in and of themselves. The concept of the schizophrenogenic or disturbance-producing family has yielded to the more sophisticated notion of several factors meshing to produce pathology. The etiology of family problems in Haley's view is not a simple one because of this or that person or because of this or that factor. It is a complex blending of various ingredients many of which are not apparent on the surface. For example, one need only think of the metacommunication which goes on beneath the surface and the concept of the double bind to see his point.

Paradigms

Seeing schizophrenia as the result of a variety of causes is surely a different way of viewing pathology. It is the result of the lens Haley uses. His paradigm is not an intrapsychic one and so his picture is likewise different because results obtained are contingent on the model used. It is not without reason that Freudian clients dream Freudian dreams and Jungian clients dream Jungian ones.

The paradigm used yields certain facts which demand specific therapeutic techniques. Interpretation and unconscious factors do not have a place in Haley's therapy because the goal is not insight. If one sees disturbance as residing in the system, then the method used to produce movement will be a technique that changes the system interaction. This is clear in the example of the bedwetting couple. The concept of disturbance was not his or hers but theirs.

This leads us to the question of "truth" in therapy. What is the true or right explanation of a particular piece of behavior? Note that the question implies an attitude which already contains a prejudice. It is based on the assumption that a thing is either right or wrong, black or white, up or down. It is based on the Western conception of truth as rational. In Haley's viewpoint this is a limited and limiting notion. The Eastern mind, on the other hand, does not see life as neatly divided into boxes, all hermetically sealed off from one another, and labeled as feeling world, rational world, and volitional world. The Zen Master does not teach his pupil by leading him from A to Z. Rather he uses paradox, and he teaches by not teaching, he leads by not leading. He asks questions like "What is the sound of one hand clapping?" And the pupil stands in awe—dumbstruck.

In therapy, the intrapsychically oriented clinician talks learnedly of psychodynamics and of oral, anal, and phallic stages of growth. Within this frame of reference he sees certain factors emerge, and he plans strategies designed to alter these factors. Similarly, the system analyst will look at the same picture and speak of interlocking pathologies, of system disturbance, of metacommunication, and so on, and get another picture of the same scene. His strategy will be different from that of his colleague, and at times, diametrically so, for example, Erickson's negative attitude toward the role of insight in therapy.

Who is right? Which one of the therapists has the correct picture? It is not a question one can answer glibly or without much thought. It can only be answered within a given frame of reference. The lens used is part of the process of seeing. The world seen through sunglasses is a subdued one in which colors are modified and brightness screened. It is otherwise with clear lenses.

Harry Stack Sullivan made many contributions to the field of therapy. Perhaps his most valuable one was the notion of the therapist as a participant observer, as part of the process he was observing. In family therapy the presence of the therapist is very significant and his presence alters the system. He is part of the field being observed. Diagnosis cannot be made without him. It is not accurate for a therapist to report that a family is hostile but more accurately he should say that " . . . the family members *are showing me* how hostile they are to each other."(22)

The differences are important. The former statement does not take into account the presence of the therapist, whereas the latter does. To use such an approach is to avoid the use of diagnostic categories and to use the context of the interaction between therapist and the family. Ecology then plays a role in Haley's concept of therapy.

Haley illustrates the importance of a model by using the example of a boy who steals an automobile.(23) The explanation offered of his behavior will depend on how one conceptualizes the unit of observation. If the boy alone is considered then his motivation is seen as the result of certain things about him and his nature. These can range from his being immoral to his need to express something symbolically through the theft. Regardless of the motivation chosen, however, he is the focal point under consideration and the one with the problem.

If the unit observed is expanded to include another, his father, for example, the motivation will be seen as relating in some way to their interaction. Perhaps one might hypothesize that the boy is acting out some unresolved problems of the father. Again whatever is decided will include both parties. If the unit is a triad, for example, child, mother, and father, then the child's behavior is interwoven with that of his parents. A therapist, and many family therapists in particular, would see the child's behavior as a way of saving the family system. Homeostasis is established when the parents can come together to help their son. In this model the motivation is involved with the system of which he is part.

It is clear that the unit chosen for observation determines not only what is seen but how it is treated. The choice made reflects the model used. It is likewise clear that Haley uses a system model and intervenes accordingly. This example should illuminate the earlier question of which model was the correct or right one. In any event it highlights the importance of theory and model building in therapy. Procedure of its nature implies a commitment to some kind of model. Just as one cannot not communicate so also one cannot not have a therapeutic model, at least implicitly. The role of model building will be treated at length in Part 3.

CRITICAL ISSUES: JAY HALEY

What Is a Family?

Haley would hold that a family is a system which involves power relations. However, he would point out that our conceptual categories still have not found appropriate terms to describe family interaction.

The interlocking relationships are noted, but we are not yet capable of adequately describing these relationships. In an interview at the Philadelphia Child Guidance Clinic on March 11, 1971, Haley stated that he anticipates seeing a change in the structuring of the family in the future:

> A family is a special kind of system because it has a history, ie, a past and a future. We cannot, therefore, restrict a family to blood relationships. The hippies are changing the way we think about families. We may yet have to consider any group with an ongoing relationship a family.

The type of system that exists in a family is a cybernetic one in which there are circular rather than linear patterns. Moreover, the system has rules by which it operates. Haley writes " . . . the family is a system which contains a governing process. However, there is not just a single governor for the system; each member functions as a governor of the others and thus the system is maintained."[15 (p 160)]

The family system is not a simple homeostatic model, as is found in the household thermostat system, which has error-activated ways of changing the range of the system, and a metagovernor, that is, one who sets the limits of the system. In the household system, the metagovernor, that is, the one who sets the system is outside of it. In the family system, however, the metagovernor is found within the system. It is at this level that the struggles which go on in families are found. Each family member tries to be the one who determines the limits of the behavior of the others. Added to this is the further complexity of subsystems in the family, for example, in-laws, and siblings.

What Should the Outcome of Family Therapy Be?

Change in the system is the only valid outcome. When the family does change the therapist accepts this and rewards the change. The therapist is only a "temporary intruder" in the system and this allows him to move in and out of the system without getting caught in it. Haley is not interested in the analysis of problems but in producing change.

> Change behavior and you change feelings. The traditional therapist gets nowhere, especially with black families, because all he does is talk about object-relations. You have to change the way they act and then you will change the way they feel. (interview)

Such a therapeutic approach is a radical departure from the usual way therapists work. Haley was adamant about changing behavior in the Philadelphia interview: "Unless the people act differently you are only playing intellectual games. Change means changing behavior."

How Does a Family Change?

As we saw above, the family changes when the system changes. This is accomplished through the medium of the therapist, who provides an educational model for the family and presents paradoxes, which force the family to act in different ways. Since the members of the family are locked into the system, it is virtually impossible for them to relate in new ways without outside help. The therapist acts in this capacity and moves the system to a new way of operating. He forces them to deal with new situations and produce new solutions. The family system then can stabilize at a different and more comfortable level then before.

One of the real differences within the same school of communication theorists is the approach to therapy. Feeling is not an essential part of Haley's system. The stress is on the power elements, almost exclusively so. Satir, on the other hand, will use the communication pattern she observes in a different way. Haley says that the therapist should observe the interactional pattern in the system and then comment on what this says about the power relations. Satir, however, says that the therapist in observing the interaction comments on what this says about the way people feel about each other. The distinction is important, and we will deal with it again in our final analysis of similarities and differences. Haley writes very little about the role of values in family therapy. He concentrates on the power alliances in the family and the metacommunicative aspects of relationships but does not usually deal with questions of ought or should. Apparently, he is content to break into the interactional patterns of the system, as it exists, and let the system itself decide what values it should have.

As one reads or talks to Haley, one gets the impression that Haley is a man who likes to move about, jabbing here or there, but always being somewhat elusive. The impression seems valid in view of the following statement:

The art of family therapy seems to be that of developing ways of siding with all family members at once, or of clearly taking sides with different factions at different times while acknowledging this, or of leaving the coalition situation ambiguous so that family members are uncertain where the therapist stands.(23)

In answer to our question on the outcome of family therapy during the March 11th Philadelphia interview, Haley replied that it should bring about change in the family system as we have seen. The kind or degree of change, however, should be determined by the family. Although Haley would not deny the importance of the therapist's value system, he does not make this an issue unless it becomes a problem for the family. Haley feels that family therapists develop a high tolerance for other points of view and other value systems. They may become a part of therapy but need not necessarily become an issue, although they are always present.

A final point should be made. Haley's emphasis on power relations sounds somewhat cold and distant to the uninitiated. Yet when one watches Haley work, a different impression is given. He exudes a warmth and friendliness that touches a family and communicates to the members his care and concern. Although Haley seems to play down the importance of feeling in working with families, he reaches them at this level and then goes beyond to a change in family interaction and behavior.

One might describe it best as an illustration of metacommunication. Although Haley talks about power relations, at the same time, he touches the family by communicating his interest. He shows his care by not caring and he shows his feelings by not feeling. Haley is an excellent example of a paradox in action.

The best summary of Jay Haley's approach to therapy has been stated by Haley:

> Whether a patient encounters a therapist alone or in company with his family, he finds himself involved in a relationship which educates him by teaching him new tactics and providing a model for new behavior. Simultaneously, he is faced with a relationship containing multiple paradoxes which force him to abandon his old behavior, since he can only deal with this relationship, or escape from it amiably by undergoing change.(24)

VIRGINIA SATIR: COMMUNICATION AND FEELING

Virginia Satir, mainly through one book *Conjoint Family Therapy*, has become one of the major forces in the field of family therapy.(2) The value in the book is mainly in the abundant illustrations she uses. Satir does not talk in abstractions but translates her basic philosophy into concrete examples.

We have placed her behind Jackson and Haley in this study because much of what she says is based on their thinking. In her writings she tends to allude more to others than developing basic theory. It is easier, therefore, in studying communication theory in family therapy, to see first the underlying concepts on which it is based, and then later to look at how these notions can be applied specifically.

In *Conjoint Family Therapy* Satir states some basic premises and elaborates with case studies. The method has advantages and disadvantages. Positively, it helps the student see how, in practice, one might go about doing family therapy. Negatively, it also can produce a sense of frustration, leaving the student asking himself how Satir arrives at a particular statement. The usual devices used by theorists, that is, citing authors, developing rational arguments for a position, and so on, are largely bypassed. However, when taken in conjunction with more theoretical positions, Satir's thinking fills up some of the *lacunae* that may exist in abstract thinking.

Satir also brings a dimension of feeling to communicational theory that helps to counterbalance its obvious intellectual base. Satir exudes warmth and caring in her therapy. In the past few years she has moved off into the wider areas of the encounter and human potential growth movements. Of all the therapists studied, she is the one most involved in the emotional or the feeling level of people.

Jackson, Haley, and Satir can be treated as communication theorists since they share the same basic theoretical approach to pathology, that is, it is caused by faulty communications. However, as we have seen, Jackson takes a cognitive approach; Haley, on the other hand, stresses the power relations in communication; and Satir emphasizes the feeling aspect of communication in the following remarks:

> There are four wrong ways people communicate. You can blame, you can placate, you can be irrelevant or you can be "reasonable." There's something incomplete about each way. The blamer leaves out what he feels about the other person, the placater leaves out what he feels about himself, the reasonable one leaves out what he feels about the subject being discussed and the irrelevant one leaves out everything.(25)

This is a good summary statement because she spells out what communication means: It is focused on feelings. It is not that cognition or control is unimportant but that feeling is central. The philosopher Descartes said: "I think, therefore, I am;" Satir says: "I feel, therefore, I am." It is a question of emphasis.

Satir is an effective therapist because she touches people where they experience hurt, that is, in their feelings. The cause of the hurt may be found in other areas, for example, a conflict of value system or an inability to execute decisions, but what is first noted is a pain in the area of emotions. To be sure Satir does not end at this level, but she does seem to begin on a feeling level and so engages the family in treatment by responding to their hurt.

The emphasis is on needs, but needs as related to emotional interchanges in the family system and not just material things. The family is the place where these kinds of needs are met. If they are not met, then symptoms begin to appear and are a clue to a disturbance in the system. The way to get to the disturbance, the underlying cause, is to attend to the here and now pain. Brains think and wills execute, but people feel pain in their emotional system. It is an obvious concept but perhaps so obvious that it is often overlooked. Satir begins with this level and proceeds to move into the family system, less in the role of expert therapist, and more as an empathic facilitator of communication.

Maturation

A basic concept for Satir is that of maturation. "The most important concept in therapy, because it is a touchstone for all the rest, is that of maturation."[2 (p 91)] The state of maturation involves two basic levels of operation: (1) The mature person is fully in charge of himself; and (2) he is one who can make choices based on accurate perceptions about himself and others and is able to take responsibility for his decisions. The patterns of behavior that mark such a mature person will be: the ability to be in touch with his own feelings; the ability to communicate with others clearly; an acceptance of others as different from himself; and a willingness to see differentness as a chance to learn and explore rather than as a threat.

The description given by Satir is strikingly similar to that of Murray Bowen's concept of differentiation of self as we shall see. Both theorists emphasize the importance of separating one's self out of the family, of becoming a clearly delineated self, and the link between an inability to do this and pathology.

Dysfunctional Communication

Opposed to this picture of the functional person is the dysfunctional or inadequate person, one who cannot separate himself out of the family mass, and is unable to give or receive clear messages. The breakdown or impairment of communication is the sign that one has become dysfunctional. "We call an individual dysfunctional when he has not learned to communicate properly."[2 (p 92)]

What causes faulty communication? Satir states that it is linked to a person's self concept. If this is poor, and one has a low sense of self-esteem, the possibility of problems of communication is high. The poor self-image, the low esteem, in turn, is attributable to the early formative relations with the family structure, with the relation to mother and father. She suggests that the parents may have been poor models of communication, or the content of their communication may have been devaluating to the child, or the parental communication itself was disturbed. Also, in a more direct way, the child's self-esteem was impaired because his developmental steps in growth were not validated.

As we can see, Satir presents a view which links the inability to separate one's self from the family with the communication system of the family. The inability to communicate is the signal that one is not functioning. This comes from a poor image of self which is formed by the interaction of the parents and the child. The message is delivered to the child that he is not what he should be. He is a disappointment, or more likely he is sick. One is reminded of Jackson's frequent observation that in certain families one who exhibits such behavior is labelled "mad" or "sick," as if the family system had nothing to do with the process. Note that Satir's position regarding communcation does not refer only to what is said but to the relational aspects, as well. She shares the same basic idea of communication theory as Jackson and Haley, that is, it is not words alone that are meant but all interactional behavior.

Satir's analysis is similar to that of the other communication theorists. For example, she speaks of a denotative or literal level of communication and also a metacommunicative level which qualifies the literal and reflects on the relationship of the persons. In this she follows the analysis given by Haley. She emphasizes, in particular, the congruency or incongruency of messages given and received. *Congruency* refers to the harmony that exists between the literal and metacommunicative levels. *Incongruency*, on the other hand, refers to the disharmony or the discrepancy between the report and command aspects of a message.

So far we have seen the role of communication in pathology, its roots in lack of self-esteem, and the role of the parents in the process of the child's poor self image. To complete our picture of Satir's system, we must look at the marital dyad and the family triad.

Marital Dyad and Family Triad

In her analysis of marital interaction, Satir ties in the fundamental concept of self-esteem which is basic to her system. She has observed that self-esteem and not sex is the basic drive in man. "From what I have observed, the sex drive is continually subordinated to and used for the purpose of enhancing self-esteem and defending against threats to self-esteem."[2 (p 55)]

Self-esteem will operate at all levels of interaction. Therefore, it will be a force in the choice of marriage partner. If a man, for example, has a strong sense of self, then he will choose as a marital partner one who will enhance his self-esteem by complementing his personality and talents. However, if he has a low self-esteem, a poor self-image, he will reach out to the other not as a complement but as one who will supply what is missing in the "self" " . . . as an extension of self . . . "[2 (p 28)]

To relate to another, especially in as intimate and demanding a relationship as marriage, is to court disaster. Such a union will be dysfunctional by its very nature. This is so because both parties look to marriage as a place of getting rather than giving. Marriage is seen as a chance to do something about one's own inadequate personality. The only outcome of such a marriage is disillusionment and an increase in feelings of negative self-esteem. Logically, one might see divorce or separation as a way of terminating the mismatch. However, more often, the birth of a child is viewed as a means of attaining the desired self-esteem. The child is seen as a way of demonstrating to the community their worth to others, or esteem for themselves as parents, or as an extension of self.

What is important here is that the child is never seen in himself as a separate person with a value and worth apart from the parent's self-esteem. The child or children are thus given a load to carry which is most difficult and burdensome. They must literally live out parental fantasies. Success or failure then is always viewed from the vantage point of the parent. Individuality or difference in outlook gets translated as a lack of love, just as it does between the parents.

In Satir's view the child is in an intolerable position as the third angle of the family triangle. Whichever way he or she turns, there is a problem. Since the parents are in conflict, any and all actions of the child will be interpreted as being for or against one or the other. This is further complicated in that by reason of sex the child is already identified with one or the other parent.

"Given this state of affairs, if the child seems to side with one parent, he runs the risk of losing the other parent. Since he needs both parents, making such a choice inevitably hurts him.''[2 (p 30)] Not only does it hurt the child in the obvious sense of making him take sides but such a choice is deleterious to psychosexual development. A child needs a parent of the same sex to identify with and a parent of the opposite sex to be admired and sought as desirable. When a child, however, is forced to choose one or the other, psychosexual development is stunted or stifled.

Satir's conceptualization of the role of the child as the identified patient follows the thinking of Lidz as we saw previously. Lidz stressed that unless there was a parental coalition, the child would be brought in by either parent to fulfill unsatisfied wishes. Satir follows his thinking on the consequences of the marital breakdown's effect on the child's role in the family.

This brings us to a consideration of the triangle itself. Here, too, Satir is in agreement with Murray Bowen's thinking. Satir holds that there is in reality no such thing as a triangular relationship, but only shifting two-person relationships. "In my opinion there is no such thing as a relationship between three people. There are only shifting two-person relationships with the third member in the role of observer."[2 (p 58)] In this viewpoint she is agreeing with Haley's analysis of what he calls perverse triangles.

Haley cites a case in which an identified patient, a daughter, was sent back home from the hospital. Immediately, the parents separated a demanded the girl make a choice between them. In point of fact, a triangle did not exist but a desire for a two-person coalition was being requested. Haley further comments that the girl " . . . was involved in a group of ten cross-generational triangles."[23 (pp 22)]

The building blocks of Satir's system are made up of a series of two-person interacting relationships. The key, however, to the success or failure of the system is the relationship of the husband and wife. If this is working reasonably well, each can allow the other to have a relationship with the child. However, when the marital dyad is dysfunctional, when the parental coalition is nonexistent, then "Both mates look to the child to satisfy their unmet needs in the marital relationship."[2 (p 58)]

The child who is triangled into the marital structure, and appears to be on one side or the other, in fact, is not happy with the role of "ersatz mate." The child has loyalties to both parents and need for both. Satir comments: "Children cannot unambivalently side with either parent."[2 (p 59)]

The final aspect to be looked at in Satir's system is the question of how one gets a sense of self-esteem. It occurs in the early development of the child and involves a variety of things. Besides the obvious physical needs, the child has need for a warm, ongoing, predictable relationship with another. There is also a need for an experience of mastery over his world. In addition, a validation of himself as a distinct and worthwhile person is needed. Finally, there is required a sense of what it is to be male or female and an acceptance of this.

These qualities can be attained only in a relationship with the parents. Satir writes:

> If parents consistently show that they consider their child a masterful, sexual person, and if they also demonstrate a gratifying, functional male-female relationship, the child acquires self-esteem and becomes increasingly independent of his parents.[2 (p 53)]

The overall impression one gets in viewing Satir's analysis of family process is that of a tightly knit, interlocking idea of how a family operates. All the pieces fit together and are connected. The conclusion to be drawn is that one cannot look just at any one part, whether that be the identified patient, or the parental coalition, or the lines of communication, or finally, the low self-esteem, as if these existed in isolation.

How this approach works in practice can be seen in the careful analysis she gives of her initial interview with the Pope family.(26) She comments there: "To understand the meaning of the symptom, I have to see how it fits into the family system. I believe that every piece of behavior in a family is logical to that system."[26 (p 98)] We can see that Satir adheres to the principle of circular feedback and homeostatic balance in the family as do all the communication theorists.

Satir implicitly has a value system which is related to the manner in which she does therapy. There are three primary beliefs about human nature:

1.   Every person is geared to survival, growth, and getting close to others. All behavior, however distorted, aims at implementing these.
2.   That what society labels as sick or crazy is an attempt to signal that one is in distress.
3.   Thought and feeling are bound together. A person can learn what he does not know and can change his way of interacting.[2 (pp 96–97)]

The model Satir is proposing is not the traditional medical model which sees an analogy between physical and mental health but what is called a *growth model*. In this model pathology is linked to the inability of a person to reach his potential for development. It has as an underlying premise the notion that human beings are geared toward fulfillment. Human nature is fundamentally good and not fundamentally evil. At the heart of her theory of doing therapy is a philosophical concept which determines the direction she will follow.

The question of a value system is one which is critical in any kind of therapy. Moreover, it grows out of the basic premises one has toward life; that is, it has its roots in metaphysica. Satir prefers to talk openly about her value system and to make such questions issues for therapy. We shall see how she deals with this in relation to the way feelings are dealt with in a family system.

Family Rules

In 1972, Satir published a sequel to *Conjoint Family Therapy*.(27) It is a book aimed not so much at family therapists as at families themselves. It is designed to spell out two things; (1) How a family can examine itself, that is, the way it functions; and (2) How it can go about making changes it deems necessary. Satir states that "All of the ingredients in a family that count are changeable and correctable . . ."[28 (p xi)]

Three of the elements which make for family process we have already seen: self-worth, communication, and system. The fourth has to do with rules. Behavior is seen as the result of the interplay of these forces.

By rules Satir means the concept of *should*. The term refers to the way business gets done in the family. Every family has rules but not all are aware of them nor do all agree on the basic meaning of each rule.

A goal of therapy therefore is to help the family find out which rules apply and which are no longer relevant. Satir, of course, is not referring only to the obvious rules in a family such as who does the dishes or who takes out the garbage. Again, as always, the focus is on feelings. What are the feeling rules which exist in a family? Are there forbidden topics? If so what are they? What are the rules, mostly covert and unwritten, that cause family pain? To understand the importance of rules in her thinking, one must recall that the model she uses is not the medical model of health or sickness but a growth model which sees symptoms not so much as entities in themselves but as the result of processes which prevent a person from growing. A person cannot attain maturity unless his capacities are allowed free play.

Rules regarding emotional interchange are not always easy to locate but unless they can be observed, they cannot be changed. A task for Satir is to make these kinds of rules known. This then permits the family to make adjustments, to add or subtract and to alter them.

The primary rule has to do with what she calls "the freedom to comment." More specifically it involves four elements: (1) The freedom to express what one is seeing or hearing; (2) Who those members are in the family to whom one can talk; (3) The freedom to disagree or disapprove; and (4) How one asks questions when one does not understand.[27 (pp 96–111)]

Each family will have its own rules. To a large extent these may be culturally conditioned. In a family a rule may be that only good things may be said and only good feelings expressed. There is a prohibition against having or expressing negative feelings. If this is so, then what does one do when one feels angry? Is it to be denied or perhaps translated into psychosomatic complaints? The question Satir asks, as most of her questions, are practical ones which have to do with day-to-day living.

The issue of rules involves the question of values. Rules always express a value system by which the family operates. Dysfunctional families will have dysfunctional rules since one begets the other. The lines of communication become crossed and symptoms begin to appear. Often the family does not know what is happening because it is not aware of the unwritten rules by which it operates.

Underneath the concept of rules is the distinction between feeling and action. Families tend to confuse the two. Satir works at making the distinction clear to family members so that each person in the family system is aware of the difference between how one feels and what one should do with such a feeling. Satir illustrates the difference by alluding to affection and sex. Affection is a feeling but sexual activity is an expression of that feeling. In many families not only is sexual activity taboo but even the feeling of affection. This may lead to problems.

Even more confusion seems to exist around the area of anger and its expression. Frequently, children are taught that they should not feel angry toward their brothers or sisters. This is unreal and produces problems. More correctly, children should be taught that negative feelings are a normal experience and are not wrong or forbidden. How these feelings get expressed is another matter. One family member may be justified in feeling angry at another, but this does not give that person a right to express the feeling in a way that is destructive. For example, Johnny, a 5-year-old may feel angry that his 3-year-old sister is being given preferential treatment, but he must learn that he cannot therefore proceed to beat up his sister. On the other hand, he should not be told that it is wrong for him to feel negatively toward his sister, as is often the case.

Satir again is focusing on feelings when she talks about rules. She is articulating a point of view which says that feelings are good, all feelings both positive and negative, but that sometimes in a family there exist rules, usually covert, which make expression of these difficult or even forbidden. The therapist has to check into the family rules and expose those that are causing pain. This gives the family the option of making changes. It gives the family the experience of control of their system. It shows them that things do not just happen but are the result of interacting forces. When these forces are labeled, they can then be changed.

A final observation is in order. Satir is a system thinker because she does not talk about "bad" people who cause the family pain. Instead she speaks about "bad" rules which cause the pain. Things are bad but not people. This distinction has great practical consequence for the therapist.

To take the label off a person and to put it on a way of interacting is to defuse a potentially volatile situation. Instead of saying that John is the cause of the family problem, saying that some rules in the family are causing a problem has a twofold effect. First, it takes the label of scapegoat off John and makes him part of the family system and not the cause of its pain. This gives him some breathing room and opens up the possibility of his changing. Second, the parents do not have to feel that they have been failures in their parental role. They have been guilty, perhaps, of overlooking certain procedures in the family, but they no longer have to feel guilty of failing as human beings. To put it more simply: they can retain their feeling of self-worth as persons and as parents.

The distinction is important because instead of locking the system into itself by reinforcing the labels of identified patient and failing parents, it opens up the possibility of change in the system. This is another instance of how theory is related to practice.

CRITICAL ISSUES: VIRGINIA SATIR

What Is a Family?

A family is a group composed of adults of both sexes who live under the same roof and have a socially acceptable sexual relationship. This group is held together by mutually reinforcing functions which include sexual needs, procreative needs, and transmitting of cultural values, especially teaching the children how to develop emotional maturity. Its goal is the nurture, support, and direction of its members. What these goals are will differ somewhat from class to class but, in general, will be those geared to survival and growth. Satir tends to play down the differences in cultural aspects, thinking they are overrated. "People are people. They come bleeding and hurt and wanting and need the same things regardless of differences in social class." (Discussion at the Nathan Ackerman Family Institute, December 1, 1970.)

Satir, however, does not minimize the importance of cultural factors. She has worked with families of different backgrounds and has done family therapy in Japan. She is cognizant of the importance of such differences. What she is emphasizing though is that for emotional survival a human being, of whatever economic or social class, needs certain basic human contacts.

Traditionally, the place where these interpersonal needs are met and gratified is in the family. The family then is the place of exchange of those things needed for growth and survival. It is not the only place where these needs are met, but it is the first place that one encounters in life. Church and school, regardless of intention, can at best reinforce what is given at home. The family is first not only chronologically, in time, but also psychologically, in importance. The family is the *matrix*, the nest, which allows for the possibility of growth or decline.

The family is the system in which various needs at different levels, physical, emotional, and cultural are met and gratified, or not. It is seen as the key unit in society because it is the place which mediates between the person and the wider society. It brings the person to society and society to the person. Its role is crucial for without an effective family system, neither society nor the person can attain their goals.

What Should the Outcome of Family Therapy Be?

"If illness is seen to derive from inadequate methods of communication . . . it follows that therapy will be seen as an attempt to improve these methods."[2 (p 96)] More specifically, there are three goals.

1. Each member should be able to report congruently, completely and obviously on what he sees and hears, feels and thinks about himself and others, in the presence of others.

2. Each person should be related to in his uniqueness so that decisions are made in terms of exploration and negotiation rather than in terms of power.
3. Differentness must be openly acknowledged and used for growth.(28)

Pathology is found in the family system and not in the individual members of it. What is communicated in that system, the information that is processed, is not being sent clearly or being received accurately. The paradigm of a communication model is obviously being used.

Satir is consistent in applying the model to the area of feeling or emotion. The emphasis is on the heart and not the head. The family system is in pain because the rules by which it operates are too constricting for growth. Satir would maintain that rules are necessary for functioning effectively but in the dysfunctional system are too rigid or too hidden. If the former is the case, the family system must adjust and allow for a change in its value system. If the latter case is true, the rules must be exposed and brought to the surface.

Peoplemaking is an attempt to explicitate the procedures by which a family might extricate itself from a dysfunctional system. This is not easily accomplished and so may require an outside intervention by one who is not part of the family system.

How Does a Family Change?

Satir says that the therapist becomes a communication model with the family members in terms of their relationship to him and to each other. Why communication? Because through it we learn the family rules, how the system operates. Specifically, we learn the rules about the following:

1. Self and manifesting it;
2. Self and the expectation of the other;
3. Self and the outside world.[28 (p 129)]

How does the therapist accomplish an explicitation of the rules? He does so by becoming a model of communication. In particular, he will teach the family the difference between the meaning given and the meaning received. Also, he teaches that one be alert for incongruent, confused, or covert messages. He does this by constantly checking out the interaction within the system and serving as the model of communication. By acting in this way he fulfills his goals of achieving clear, congruent, and reality based communication among all family members.

Although it is theoretically possible for a family system to correct itself, usually in practice it is necessary to have a therapist to effect change. The detachment from the system required for observing it and then moving to alter it is beyond the capabilities of most families.

The therapist does not labor under these handicaps. He can observe lines of communication and make comments about them. He has both an expertise in communication and a freedom from the system that gives him a leverage powerful enough to move it. The therapist is a teacher and a model. He leads a family into new ways of thinking and behaving. He does this not only by talking but more effectively by modeling. He does not just talk about communication, he demonstrates it in his relationship to the family system. He responds to it, especially on a feeling level, and shares with it his own world. He is not distant and aloof but a model of warmth and empathy yet able to confront when necessary.

The goal of his work is to foster those conditions which allow for emotional growth. Each person is individual, a unique kind of being, who to flower must attain a sense of self-worth or self-esteem. This is the ultimate goal, and the role of the therapist is to help the family system, the *matrix* out of which the conditions for growth are found, to flourish. Without a caring family system the individual will not attain self-esteem.

Note that there is a similarity in the theoretical concepts of Satir on the need for others to gain self-esteem, and the psychoanalytic concept of object-relations where the ego is seen as the center of the personality reaching out to objects for support.

The concept of object-relations is a departure from the classical Freudian view in that it emphasizes the role of the ego. Ronald Fairbairn, a British analyst who developed the notion, sees the mother-child relationship as critical.(29) His study of schizoid personalities led him to postulate that their inability to make or maintain ongoing relationships could be traced to a poor initial interrelationship between mother and child. Given this theoretical frame of reference, it follows that therapy will be a process by which the client experiences the therapeutic relationship as a second chance to form good object-relations.

Satir's frame of reference is not too dissimilar although her language is. The family is the *matrix* out of which the personality grows and reaches its potential. It is the place where one is recognized and the concept of self-esteem and self-worth begins to grow. If this familial experience is hurtful, however, the developing personality is stunted and becomes fearful of future involvement. In her view this is caused by faulty communication of the importance and value of a person to that individual family member.

Therapy then will be a process in which the therapist becomes the model of communication freeing the family system to interact in a way that leads to growth. We will again pick up this notion of object-relations in family therapy when we speak about some current trends in the field.

NOTES AND REFERENCES

1. Bateson G, Jackson D, Haley J, Weakland J: Toward a theory of schizoprenia, Jackson D (ed): in Communication, Family, and Marriage. Palo Alto, Science and Behavior Books, 1968, pp 31–54
2. Satir V: Conjoint Family Therapy (ed 2). Palo Alto, Science and Behavior Books, 1967, p 96
3. Watzlawick P, Beavin J, Jackson D: Pragmatics of Human Communication. New York, Norton, 1967, p 48 ff
4. Haley J: Uncommon Therapy, New York, Norton, 1973
5. Jackson D, Yalom I: Conjoint family therapy as an aid to intensive psychotherapy, Burton A (ed): in Modern Psychotherapeutic Practice. Palo Alto, Science & Behavior Books, 1965, p 80–98
6. Jackson D, Weakland J: Schizophrenic Symptoms and Family Interaction. Arch Gen Psychiatry 1:618–621, 1959
7. Jackson D. The question of family homeostasis, in Jackson D (ed): Communication, Family, and Marriage. Palo Alto, Science & Behavior Books, 1968, pp 1–2
8. Hall A, Fagen D: Definition of a system. General Systems Yearbook I:18–28, 1956
9. Jackson D: Family Rules: The Marital Quid Pro Quo. Arch Gen Psychiatry 12:589–594, 1965
10. Albee E: Who's Afraid of Virginia Woolf?. New York, Pocket Books, 1964
11. Lederer W, Jackson D: The Mirages of Marriage. New York, Norton, 1968
12. Jackson D: The Eternal Triangle, Haley J, Hoffman L (eds): in Techniques of Family Therapy, New York, Basic Books, 1967, pp 174–264
13. Jackson D, Weakland J: Conjoint family therapy: Some considerations on theory, technique, and results. Psychiatry 24:30–45, 1961

A good summary article of how Jackson uses theory in practice.
14. Haley J: The power tactics of Jesus Christ, in The Power Tactics of Jesus Christ. New York, Grossman Publications, 1969, p 36
15. Haley J: Strategies of Psychotherapy. New York, Grune & Stratton, 1963, p 4
16. Haley J: Observation of the Family of the Schizophrenic. Am J Orthopsychiatry 30: 1960, 460

17. Haley J: An Interactional Description of Schizophrenia. Psychiatry 22: 1959, 323
18. Haley J: The control of fear with hypnosis. Am J Clin Hypnosis 2:114–115, 1960
19. Erickson M: Indirect hypnotherapy of a bedwetting couple, in Haley J (ed): Changing Families. Grune & Stratton, 1971, pp 65–68
20. Haley J: A review of the family therapy field, in Haley J (ed): Changing Families. New York, Grune & Stratton, 1971, p 8
21. Haley J: Approaches to family therapy, in Haley J (ed): Changing Families. New York, Grune & Stratton, 1971, p 231
22. Haley J: Family therapy: A radical change, in Haley J (ed): Changing Families. New York, Grune & Stratton, 1971, pp 277–278
23. Haley J: Toward a theory of pathological systems, in Zuk G, Boszormen-yi-Nagy I (eds): Family Therapy and Disturbed Families. Palo Alto, Science & Behavior Books, 1967, p 26
24. Haley J: Whither family therapy? In the Power Tactics of Jesus Christ. New York, Grossman Publications, 1969, p 117
25. Howard J: Please Touch. New York, McGraw-Hill, 1970, pp 149–150
26. Satir V: A family of angels, in Haley J, Hoffman L (eds): Techniques of Family Therapy. New York, Basic Books, 1967 pp 97–173
27. Satir V: Peoplemaking. Palo Alto, Science & Behavior Books, 1972
28. Satir V: The family as a treatment unit, in Haley J (ed): Changing Families. New York, Grune & Stratton, 1971, p 130
29. Fairbairn WRD: An Object-Relations Theory of the Personality. New York, Basic Books, 1954

8

Murray Bowen

The thinking of Murray Bowen has developed over the years through a process of refining basic concepts.(1) Beginning with analysis, moving on to work with married couples, and finally to dealing with family systems, Bowen has traced his thought in a series of articles in professional journals and at various symposia on family therapy. This journey he has called a process from couch to coach, from analysis to a system model.(2)

EARLY STUDIES IN SCHIZOPHRENIA

Bowen began his study of schizophrenia in 1954 in association with other colleagues, notably Warren Brodey.(3) They made a study of hospitalized families each with a schizophrenic member. The families lived in the hospital from 6 months to 2.5 years. They were characterized by a number of qualities most notable of which were:

1. They were restrictive in their relationships.
2. The concept of roles was stereotyped.
3. They made selective use of the external, i.e., only insofar as it validated their inner projection.

The initial working hypothesis conceptualized schizophrenia as a " ... psychopathological entity in the patient which had been influenced to a principle degree by the mother."(4) Bowen felt that an

107

unresolved, symbiotic attachment to the mother was the basic problem of the patient. Then the role of the father was considered.(5) Shortly thereafter, the hypothesis was extended, because of clinical observation, to the whole family. Bowen was now in the process of moving from the traditional intrapsychic approach toward a system analysis, going from the mother to the father to the whole family. Within a short time, Bowen added another dimension—the role of the grandparents:

> . . . the grandparents were relatively mature but their combined immaturities were acquired by one child who was most attached to the mother. When this child married a spouse with an equal degree of immaturity, and when the same process repeated itself in the third generation, it resulted in one child (the patient) with a high degree of immaturity, while the other siblings are much more mature.[4 (p 354)]

Here, Bowen is saying that schizophrenia is not a disease entity as such, an isolated phenomenon, but the result of an ongoing process whose history can be traced.

How does this process, begun with the grandparents, develop into an identified schizophrenic patient in the grandchildren? Bowen says it is caused by a bad relationship with the parents in the second generation. Clinically, he observes that the parents of schizophrenic offspring have poor marriages. They are characterized by a quality of interaction that Bowen labels as an "emotional divorce." This he describes as " . . . a marked emotional distance between the parents."[4 (p 354)]

Bowen believes the marital pair has picked up certain undesirable traits from their parents. They come into marriage themselves with unresolved conflicts. Marriage, and the intimacy it necessitates, make these conflicts more intense. The marital partners, unable to handle their feelings and problems, try to settle these by distancing from one another. Frequently, this gives a facade that the marriage is a happy one because it is not marked by open quarreling and dispute. Nevertheless, beneath the surface, there is a struggle. When a child is born into such a marital dyad, it becomes an interdependent triad. Bowen says that the child cannot escape from the triad so that the father, mother, and child are locked into the family oneness.

Within this system there are a variety of combinations. Bowen observes that the most common pattern " . . . is one in which the mother . . . has the 'custody' of the patient, while the father is distant and passive."(6)

Since the parents cannot relate in a meaningful way, the child gets "triangled" into the system. This means that the child becomes the focus of the relationship and therefore cannot escape. The child is locked into the system and finds it virtually impossible to leave the family. The therapist must strive to get the family to focus on itself as the problem rather than the identified patient and, hopefully, to get the members to work together.

From this work with schizophrenic families, Bowen draws two conclusions: first, the schizophrenic psychosis of the identified patient is only a symptom of a pathological family system; second, the identified patient's pathology can be seen and understood only in relation to the emotional system of which he is part. In other words, there is an emotional contagion in the family and the identified patient is the one who carries the label "sick," whereas, in fact, the emotional system itself is sick.

What is significant about these observations is the transfer between schizophrenic families and other more "normal" kinds of families. Bowen maintains that the same factors are operating in all families, but to a lesser extent. Nevertheless, he would feel that his observations can be applied to any family system, and are of importance in our study of family therapy. He writes: "It was surprising to find that all the family dynamisms so striking in schizophrenia were also present in families with the least severe problems and even in "normal" or asymptomatic families."(7)

We classify Bowen among the system people because he accepts the idea that the family is a system, that is, a change in one part will necessarily produce a change in another part. In fact, the family is any number of systems and subsystems. However, Bowen is interested in the family from a therapeutic viewpoint as an "emotional relationship system." He writes: "The term emotional refers to the force that motivates the system and relationship to the ways it is expressed. Under relationship would be subsumed communication, interaction, and other relationship modalities."(8)

However, we can see that Bowen is not to be classified with the communication theorists because he views communication as part of a wider system of relationships. In his theoretical concepts Bowen regards pathology as something very deep within man·that has its roots in biology. Bowen writes as follows:

I view emotional illness as a much deeper phenomenon than that conceptualized by current psychological theory. There are emotional mechanisms as automatic as a reflex and that occur as predictably as the force that causes the sunflower to keep its face towards the sun. I believe that the laws that govern man's emotional functioning are as orderly as those that govern other natural systems. . . .[8 (p 170)]

Bowen makes a further distinction between an "emotional system" and a "feeling system." He continues:

Operationally I regard an emotional system as something deep that is in contact with cellular and somatic processes, and a feeling system as a bridge that is in contact with parts of the emotional system on one side and with the intellectual system on the other.[8 (p 170)]

UNDIFFERENTIATED FAMILY-EGO MASS

The central concept in Bowen's theory is the "undifferentiated family-ego mass." By this he means a quality of "stuck togetherness" or fusion which is " . . . a conglomerate emotional oneness that exists in all levels of intensity."[8 (p 171)] This quality of "stuck-togetherness" exists in families at varying degrees of intensity from extremely so to very slight. However, it is a characteristic which belongs to all families, which is why Bowen feels it is central. Time is an important dimension too. When stress and tension are at high levels the intensity of the "ego mass" may increase. Members of a family may even come to know feelings, fantasies, and dreams experienced by other members. The process then is cyclical having a series of phases in which the "ego mass" becomes more or less intense. Bowen writes:

Theoretically, the fusion is present to some degree in all families except those in which family members have attained complete emotional maturity. In mature families, individual family members are contained emotional units who do not become involved in emotional fusions with others.[7 (p 219)]

How does the "family-ego mass" get started? What is the basic building block of Bowen's system? Bowen writes " . . . The basic building block of any emotional system is the 'triangle.' "[8 (p 185)] He says that when the tension between two persons in the system goes beyond a certain point, the system "triangles" in a third person, in order that the tension shift within the system. Bowen holds that "An emotional system is composed of a series of interlocking triangles." [8 (p 185)]

The importance of "triangles" as building blocks will become clearer when we talk about the aims of family therapy. It is sufficient for now to observe that the family system, the "undifferentiated family-ego mass," gets built through an ongoing process of interlocking triangles.

SIX INTERLOCKING CONCEPTS

The notion of the undifferentiated family-ego mass which Bowen initially observed in the 1950s has been refined over the past 20 years. Some suggest that his entire system is made up of six interlocking concepts:

1. Differentiation of self-scale
2. Nuclear family emotional system
3. Family projection process
4. Multigenerational transmission process
5. Sibling position profiles
6. Triangles(9)

The first element to be considered has to do with how one separates himself out from his family of origin. This notion is contrasted with its opposite, undifferentiation or fusion. Bowen conceptualizes a way of describing and distinguishing human functioning along a continuum. It may be represented by the diagram in Figure 3.

Fig. 3.   The Differentiation of self scale.

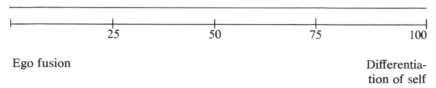

Ego fusion   Differentia-
                                                                tion of self

The scale in Figure 3 is divided into four quadrants. At the lower end of the scale, there is almost no differentiation of self. People in this category live in a feeling world and are almost wholly dependent on the feelings of those around them. In the second quadrant, there is more differentiation of self and less fusion with others, but still the quality of "stuck-togetherness" dominates. These people are able to function but in a limited way because of their fusion. Those between 50 and 75 are more able to take an "I" position and rely less on the judgment of others. Those in the highest quadrant are very rare people who represent an almost total emotional maturity and who function at a high level of independence. Bowen notes one does not meet such people in clinical practice and only on occasion socially.[8 (p 175)]

A second theoretical concept has to do with the nuclear family emotional system and the outside emotional forces which affect it. These include the extended family, work situations, and social factors that chart the course of the process within the family-ego mass. These outside factors actually influence the intensity and the extent of the emotional process in the family-ego mass.

The marital couple, in Bowen's experience, uses three major ways of controlling the intensity of the ego fusion within the family ego mass. The first is marital conflict. When this occurs, each spouse will fight for an equal share of the common self and neither will give in to the other. A second way of controlling intensity is a dysfunction in one of the spouses. This happens after conflict and one of the two will give in to the other. The one who gives in will then become very dependent on the other person, and often be labeled "sick," manifesting a variety of physical and emotional problems. The third way used is the transmission of the problem to one or more of the children. The child becomes the focal point of the problem and functions for a time but eventually breaks down under the burden of carrying the family.

This third way is so important and so common that Bowen says it exists in all families to some degree so that it is treated as a separate concept. It refers to how the parental undifferentiation is projected onto one or more children. The family projection process is the result of parental immaturity. The reason why this or that child is focused on in a given family is not always easily evident since the process may occur for a variety of reasons connected with the developmental stages of the marriage.(10)

But if one accepts a developmental notion in marriage, then the family projection process makes much more sense, so that the choice of a child is less capricious than at first glance. One might add further that clinically it is frequently observed that a child in a family not only is nominated for such a role but often "runs for the job," that is, actively seeks the role of scapegoat. Even though one can say that such behavior is self-defeating, nevertheless, the "victim" does get his strokes, albeit negative ones. From his point of view it may be better to be scapegoated than to be neglected.

Such a child will be the " . . . one most emotionally attached to the parents, and the one who ends up with a lower level of differentiation of self."[9 (p 122)] It will be more difficult for such a child "to escape" from the family because he will be more involved in it; the quality of adhesiveness, of overcloseness, of stickiness, of stuck-togetherness will be more evident in him than in his siblings.

The next concept is the multigenerational process by which

transmission takes place. For example, a fairly extended period of time is needed for a person to arrive at the level of "no self" which characterizes the schizophrenic. It is a phenomenon that does not occur overnight.

This concept is a natural corollary of concept one concerning the differentiation of self scale. The choice of a marriage partner is not accidental, but related to where one is on the scale. It has been noted that "The life style of a person at one level is so different from someone only a few points removed on the scale, they do not choose each other for personal relationships."[9 (p 120)] Since it is out of personal relationships that marital partners are chosen, it follows that a spouse chooses more or less at his or her own level of differentiation. In practice, this means that a man less differentiated than his parents will choose a woman at his level. If their children do not reach their level of differentiation of self, the process moves further back down the scale. Obviously the process can go in the opposite direction as well so that movement in both directions is possible.

The practical aspect of this seemingly abstract concept can be seen in that the role of the grandparents is important in understanding current pathology in a grandchild. The process of moving up and down the scale accounts for the presence or absence of symptomatology. Health or sickness is not found in the study of a person in isolation but within the context of his family, and this includes the extended family reaching through several generations.

Sibling position is a concept Bowen has borrowed from Walter Toman.(11) The idea of birth position is not a new one. There is much folklore about it. For example, the oldest child is supposed to suffer from anxiety because he is the pace setter in the family; the youngest child is said to be spoiled; and then there is the "middle child syndrome."

In Bowen's thinking the sibling concept becomes much more sophisticated. It is related to concept three on family projection process. The child selected by the parents, the one who is most fused into the family system, will be the one who is the most infantile or immature regardless of chronology in the family. A knowledge of where a parent fitted into his own family of origin becomes important as to what is now going on within the current family system.

The concept of triangle is " ... the basic building block or "molecule" of an emotional system," writes Bowen.[1 (p 190)] This is true whether the system is family, social, or a work system. When a system involves four or more people, that system is made up of a series of interlocking triangles.

As Bowen conceives interaction, when the relationship between two people in a system gets uncomfortable, one of them will triangle in a third party. This relieves the tension between the two. Numerous examples of this can be found. For example, in *The Glass Menagerie*, as noted earlier Laura is triangled in between her mother and brother. (12) In *Who's Afraid of Virginia Woolf?*, when the relationship between George and Martha gets "too hot," the fantasized son is triangled in to reduce the pressure.(13)

What one observes then are two people who are not relating and who bring in a third party to reestablish the homeostatic balance. However, such relationships are not stable. Bowen suggests that when things are going well, are "cool," the positions are two people who are comfortable and one outsider. The latter does not like his position and so predictably moves toward one or another person in the favored position. This, of course, brings about a new balance so that one who was an outsider is now an insider and the other party is now the outsider. On the other hand, when things get "hot," being the outsider is the preferred position. In either case it is clear why Bowen speaks of the triangles as shifting and moving. Outsiders, too, are not immune from the process of triangulation as most marriage counselors can attest. The act itself of going to a marriage counselor can sometimes produce a feeling of change in the marital relationship. This is attributed to a shift in the triangle with the counselor playing one of the roles.

Having seen the basic concepts of Bowen, especially that of the triangle and its function in a family system, we now turn to the way in which the family system can change. This process is called detriangulation.

DETRIANGULATION

As we have just seen the building blocks of any emotional system are the interlocking triangles. Therefore, the process of differentiation involves a detriangling of the triangle. Bowen lists three specific ways this can be done. First, the best way is for a marital pair to do this in the presence of a potential triangle (the therapist) who remains emotionally detached. The couple cannot use or manipulate the therapist and make him part of the triangle by getting him on his or her side. A second way of doing this is to work alone with a therapist. At times, this may be the only possible way of doing therapy if other significant people in the system are unwilling or unable to be present. The third way occurs when the therapist acts as a coach from the sidelines. This is not as good because the impact of the triangle is lost, and the chances of bogging down are much greater.[8 (p 185)]

We have seen the core concept, differentiation of self from the family ego mass, and we have seen how this might be done. There is now one final question, namely, What is accomplished by this process or what is the goal of Bowen's system?

A person is born into a family system and gets involved in it through a process of triangling. He gets differentiated out of it by reversing the process, by detriangling so that he can learn to relate to others by responding not by reacting. This allows him to relate to others freely in a person to person manner.(2)

The distinction between reacting and responding is one that Bowen regards as critical. One reacts when another controls his behavior so that he is not doing what he himself wants but what the other person wants. To respond, on the other hand, means that the other person's position is taken into account but is not the cause of one's own behavior. It is the difference between being manipulated and being free. A central aim of Bowenian therapy is to enable a person to get to a position where he can respond to a system and not just react, that is, get caught in the system.

CRITICAL ISSUES: MURRAY BOWEN

What Is a Family?

A family is a complex entity made up of a series of interlocking systems and subsystems. Basically, the family is an emotional relationship system whose roots are found in the biological nature of man. Moreover, to understand a given nuclear family, it is necessary to delve into the family of origin. In an initial interview, Bowen wants to get as much information as possible before planning treatment. Such history taking is needed for a formulation about the overall patterns of functioning in the family ego mass for at least two generations.

The history taking is detailed and careful. Often, the place to begin is with the onset of the symptoms to see if they are related to other events in the nuclear or extended family. A second area of concern is the parental functioning since marriage. All things are grist for the mill and related to the family. Bowen writes:

The internal functioning is influenced by events such as closeness or distance and emotional contact with extended families, changes in residence, the purchase of a home, and occupational success or failure.[8 (p 182)]

The birth of children also causes important changes. This is most clear in the birth of the first child. The dyad has now become a triad, and the amount of psychic energy in the system will have to be redistributed.

Then the two extended families are examined to find out what kind of emotional fields these people experienced. How close or distant were their parents to their own families? Bowen, at various times, mentions that he has been impressed by Toman's notions on the order of birth of the siblings and regards this as an important dimension.

As is evident, history taking is an important part of Bowen's approach. However, it is always related to the family's "stuck togetherness." The material gathered is not looked on as yielding information about the person but about the family. Of all the theorists we have analyzed, Bowen is the one most thoroughly engrossed in the family process. Everything he does revolves around it.

Bowen would answer that a family is everything. It is the *matrix* out of which people come. The only way to understand symptomatic behavior is by a thorough examination of the nuclear and the extended family. For Bowen all data gets processed through a system, the family, and it is crucial for therapy to understand the patterns by which the data was processed.

What Should the Outcome of Family Therapy Be?

Bowen states the outcome clearly: "The basic effort of this therapeutic system is to help individual family members toward a higher level of differentiation of self."[8 (p 184)] More specifically, as we saw above, helping a person respond to the system and not just react. The ideal man is one who is inner-directed and establishes his own goals and assumes full responsibility for his life. A person with a sense of being inner-directed can relate to others, not out of need but out of strength. He no longer gets caught in a relationship of "stuck togetherness." This freedom, gained in the family, allows one to stay free of the contagion of fusion in any system of which he might be part. He is not only free in relation to his family but in all relations.

How Does a Family Change?

It is obvious that the family changes when the interlocking triangles change. That this is extremely difficult to do without outside help seems evident. Some kind of outside intervention is required. A family therapist is needed. If both spouses are willing to work on the relationship, and this is the best approach if possible, Bowen has four specific functions for the therapist to perform:

1. Defining and clarifying the relationship between the spouses,
2. Keeping self detriangled from the family emotional system,
3. Teaching the functioning of emotional systems, and
4. Demonstrating differentiation by taking "I position" stands during the course of therapy.[1 (p 193)]

At one time, Bowen worked on the communication of feelings and the analysis of the unconscious as manifested in dreams. He now works on helping people separate out their fantasy, feeling, and thinking systems. In this way the person gets to know himself and also the self of the other.[8 (p 186)]

The person learns, in Bowen's system, not to spend energy in attacking the partner but to shore up his own poorly defined ego boundaries. It means learning to respond and not react. If one spouse can do this, then it forces the other to relate at a higher level of maturity.

Perhaps the most striking feature of Bowen's conception of the therapist is his insistence that he be detached from the system. He must disengage himself by " . . . staying out of the transference."[8 (p 164)] Here Bowen would go against some other therapists who would insist that the role of the therapist was to get involved in the system. For example, Ackerman would maintain that " . . . the therapist must dive in."(14)

Another salient point is the therapist as teacher. Bowen emphasizes this more than most therapists both in theory and practice. He requires his students to detriangulate themselves from their own family system and to take the "I" position. He feels that only in this way can they teach others to do the same. Learning to be a therapist is basically undergoing the process of working on one's own family system and experiencing the difference between "responding" and "reacting." Having done this for one's self, Bowen feels the therapist can teach others how to do it.

Bowen's theory can be summarized briefly. A person begins life as part of an undifferentiated family ego mass, and in the course of time must learn to establish his own identity, to separate himself out from that family. This means working on various triangles that exist in the family system. His approach offers a viable option to a person between the frequently observed positions of anger and guilt in a family. By means of detriangulation, one can avoid the classic hassle of the adult in a family system: to stay and be angry or to leave and be guilty.(15)

Bowen says that one can stay in contact with a family of origin and thus avoid guilt, and yet at the same time, learn to respond and not react to its pressures and so avoid anger. The emphasis is on the learning aspect of this process. It is not easy to do as family forces are so deeply rooted and are centripetal. However, for one who succeeds in this process, there is a great sense of accomplishment. To differentiate one's self from another, to establish clearly marked ego boundaries is for Bowen " . . . equivalent to our familiar concept of a mature person."[7 (p 220)] This means that one is able to relate to others, especially in the family system, in meaningful ways without being fused or joined to them. One is emotionally free and can choose to move near without absorption and withdraw without guilt.

Murray Bowen's approach to family therapy seems to be gaining adherents. Over the years Bowen has trained a large number of psychiatrists throughout the country. In addition, the annual symposium conducted by Bowen at Georgetown offers a platform for his ideas.(16) Unlike some other approaches, Bowen's system offers a model which can be taught. It seems to depend less on the idiosyncratic talents or charisma of the therapist and therefore offers a more workable frame of reference than some other approaches.

Perhaps more than any other theorist, Bowen is saying something relevant to all of us. The process of differentiation of self is not restricted to certain people but is necessary for all. The difference between differentiation and fusion is one's place on a continuum. The process of detriangulation then is not restricted to "sick" people or "sick" families but applies to all. For Bowen, we are all somewhere on the continuum and all in need of becoming more differentiated.

Like others who adhere to a system approach, Bowen is dissatisfied with a terminology which reflects old models and paradigms. He writes: "As we move more and more into systems thinking and the effort to modify the family emotional system, old terms are inaccurate and we do not yet have the terms to take their place."[1 (p 202)]

Bowen's thrust, and perhaps his appeal to so many in the field of family therapy, is that he is in the vanguard of creating new terminology to replace the old. He has gone beyond therapy as we have known it. Bowen proposes, at least implies, a metapsychology which has attracted many followers and made him a major force in family therapy.

NOTES AND REFERENCES

1. Bowen M: Principles and techniques of multiple family therapy, in Bradt J, Moynihan C (eds): Systems Therapy. Washington, D.C. 1971 pp 187–203
2. Bowen M: From couch to coach. Address given at the Georgetown Univer. Symp Fam Psychotherapy, October 30, 1970
3. Brodey W: Some family operations and schizophrenia. Arch Gen Psychiatry 1:379–402, 1959
4. Bowen M: A family concept of schizophrenia, in Jackson D (ed): The Etiology of Schizophrenia. New York, Basic Books, 1960, p 348
5. Bowen M: Dysinger R, Basamania B: The role of the father in the family environment of the schizophrenic patient. Am J Psychiatry 115:1017–1020, 1959
6. Bowen M: Family psychotherapy. Am J Orthopsychiatry 31:48, 1961
7. Bowen M: Family psychotherapy with schizophrenia in the hospital and in private practice, in Boszormenyi-Nagy I, Framo J (eds): Intensive Family Therapy, New York, Harper & Row, 1965, p 216
8. Bowen M: The use of family theory in clinical practice, in Haley J (ed): Changing Families. New York, Grune & Stratton, 1971, p 169
9. Anonymous: Toward the differentiation of a self in one's own family, in Framo J (ed): Family Interaction: A Dialogue Between Family Researchers and Family Therapists. New York, Springer, 1972, pp 111–173

   The anonymous author of this article prefaces his attempt to differentiate himself from his family with a section on basic underlying concepts. These concepts reflect an approach which can easily be applied to Bowen's thinking although the author does not cite him.
10. Grunebaum H, Bryant C: The theory and practice of the family diagnostic. Part II. Theoretical aspects and resident education, Cohen I (ed): in Family Structure, Dynamics, and Therapy. Washington, Psych Research Repts APA, 1966 pp 150–162

    The notion of stages of development in marriage is fairly widely accepted. This article uses such a concept.
11. Toman W. Family Constellation. New York, Springer, 1961
12. Williams T: The Glass Menagerie. New York, New Directions 1966
13. Albee E: Who's Afraid of Virginia Woolf? New York, Pocket Books 1964
14. Ackerman N: Family interviewing: The study process, in Ackerman N, Lieb J, Pearce J (eds): Family Therapy in Transition. Boston, Little, Brown, 1970, p 5

15. Bowen and his followers are intrigued by the movie *I Never Sang for My Father* which is shown often at their meetings. It presents a situation in which an adult male wants to leave his parents and marry but feels guilty about doing so particularly after the mother dies. Eventually, he does go but with evident grief and guilt. The son did not understand family systems and did not know how to extricate himself from his.

16. The first symposium was held in May 1965 with about 40 people in attendance, The October 1973 one had well over 1,000 people present.

Summary of Part II

We have seen how family therapy began in the 1950s, starting with the notion of conceptualizing dysfunction as residing in a family system and not in a given person. The early attempts at charting the process resulted in new terminology growing out of the new paradigm or model. The double bind, pseudomutuality, schism and skew, and mystification were some of the terms invented during this time to capture the interactional dynamics.

During the next decade several major figures emerged with Ackerman being the most prominent. On the West Coast a series of people began to look more closely at communicational patterns within systems and to devise new techniques for producing change. Ackerman observed patterns of interaction which he labelled as "interlocking pathologies." He then produced the first major work in the field and continued to write throughout the 1960s. In addition, with Jackson he began the magazine *Family Process*.

On the West Coast, Jackson began to research the communicational patterns within systems and together with others, most notably Satir and Haley, to devise new techniques of producing movement in systems. In Washington, Bowen started with a basic observation that schizophrenic families seemed too attached to each other and had a quality of stuck togetherness about them. Bowen's research developed from this one characteristic into a full-fledged system of interaction and earned him a large following.

Part II has been condensed into a digestible form by seeing how the seminal ideas of family therapy, uncovered in the 1950s, developed during the next decade. It is my contention that the basic issues of family therapy focus on three questions regarding the nature of the family system, the expected outcome of therapy, and the role of the therapist in that process. These questions are all related and flow from one another. From the answers, we can get a clear picture of the similarities and differences among our major thinkers.

It is time now to put things more into perspective by comparing the seminal thinkers on the three critical issues and then along a series of dimensions related to both theoretical concepts and to practice.

PART III

A Comparison of Theorists

In Part II, we saw an overall picture of the basic thinking of the five major theorists in family therapy. Underlying these theoretical concepts was a basic approach to life. In particular, we were concerned with three specific questions relating to the nature of the family, the meaning of change and the role of the therapist in that process.

In Part III, we will examine the role of theory in family process and then compare our major theorists along a continuum relating to eight important dimensions in family therapy.

Theory and practice should be interrelated. Without the former a therapist is working by instinct alone; without the latter the therapist is living in an ivory tower. Ideally, there should be an interplay between the two.

My contention is that any theorist, of whatever school, implicitly has a theory which he follows. Certain behaviors are encouraged because of a theoretical frame of reference. Certain other behaviors are discouraged because of the same framework. We noted earlier that oft repeated observation that Freudian clients have Freudian dreams and Jungian clients have Jungian dreams. The reason should now be clear: the client picks up the messages sent by the therapist. Certainly, the Freudian analyst does not sit down and instruct his client in the kinds of material he should produce, and yet, undeniably, the client begins to produce the material that is desired. Having spent some time looking at nonverbal communication, the reason should now be more evident why this is so.

Family therapy like any form of psychotherapy is not an exact science since there are too many variables to take into account, not the least of which is the personality of the therapist. However, if family therapy is to grow, it must seriously consider the demands of the researcher. Family therapy should have a rationale for its procedures. Theory building is part of this process and not some extra to be added on to what one does.

From 1960 to 1970 a new phenomenon took root in America, the development of "encounter groups," "growth groups," "T-Groups." The names varied but the goal was a common one of growth of the individual member. The concept was noble and sometimes even its execution, but frequently the leaders of such groups did not have an idea of what they wanted to accomplish nor how they might go about attaining their goals. A good idea, a good concept had been damaged because the practice of such groups proliferated beyond the ability of people to theorize about their structure, meaning, or purpose.(1)

Similarly, during the same decade, family therapy began to make its impact felt. Conventions began to welcome papers on family process into the therapeutic arena. Demonstrations, both with live families and simulated ones, attracted large gatherings and sustained enough interest for their results to be published.(2) Universities and medical schools introduced classes or seminars in family therapy, often, grudgingly. In a word family therapy became respectable during the 1960 to 1970 decade.

Doubtlessly, family therapy had made an impact as many of its pioneers were men and women blessed with therapeutic ingenuity. Also like any great idea its time had come and many people in the field were open to receive it.

Family therapists as a group have been aware of the importance of research and have tried dutifully to bring research and practice (strange bedfellows) together. The mating of the two (sometimes stormy, sometimes productive) has been of benefit to each. The clinician who wants "to get on with helping families" needs the researcher to remind him of his underlying assumptions and premises; and the researcher, constructing theory, often on meager samples, needs the clinician to remind him that life does not always, or usually, fit into neat categories.(3)

In Part III then, we will see why theory is necessary, what theory has produced, and finally, what the similarities and the differences are in our major theorists as a result of their underlying theory of family and its function.

NOTES AND REFERENCES

1. Lieberman M, Yalom I, Miles M: Encounter Groups: First Facts. New York, Basic Books, 1973

    Especially Chapter 5 "Hazards of Encounter Groups," pp 167–210
2. Sager C, Brayboy T, Waxonberg B: Black Ghetto Family in Therapy: A Laboratory Experience. New York, Grove Press, 1970
3. Framo J: Family Interaction: A Dialogue between Family Researchers and Family Therapists. New York, Springer, 1972

    Especially Framo's "Charge to the Conference," pp 6–12

9

The Role of Theory and Type of Model Used in Family Therapy

THE ROLE OF THEORY

At this point in our study of family therapy, the reader should be asking himself some questions. Who is right? Are the concepts of Ackerman correct, or not? Or are the communication people closer to the truth? If so, which one of them? And what about Bowen's point of view? It is clear there are similarities and differences between these viewpoints. What accounts for these things? Are the differences, for example, real, or are they mainly semantic? The answers to these questions can be found in the role of theory.

One starts with a way of seeing the world. It can be called a number of things. A sociologist will speak of a frame of reference. A philosopher will talk about a *Weltanschauung*, a world view of reality. More simply we have used the idea of a lens. In any case all the terms are trying to express the way life is seen or structured. To see what is in the foreground or in the background is not just a matter of opening one's eyes and looking. What I look at, and consequently what I see, is determined by the model I am using.

In Part I, the theorists stressed the role of general system theory (GST) in the development of family therapy. GST offered a model which was different from that of the work model on which Freud and his successors based their findings.

Whereas the old model looked at what went on inside a person as the result of internal processes, the new model stated that when a piece of behavior was the result of an interaction within a system (complexes

128

of elements standing in interaction), the phenomenon observed could not be attributed to any single member of the system.

What was observed was the result of the model used. The issue is critical for understanding the nature of family therapy. To illustrate: an identified schizophrenic begins to act in a bizarre manner whenever he is sent home. Using model one the logical question to ask is: "I wonder what is going on within X which causes this behavior?" Using model two the logical question to ask is: "I wonder what kinds of things are going on in X's family system which produce this behavior?" The model used will determine the nature of the questions.

Step 1 in family therapy began with some observable facts concerning schizophrenia. Therapists noted in various geographical locations, as we have seen, that when hospitalized schizophrenic patients returned to their families within a short space of time, frequently they had to be rehospitalized. Using a system model, researchers such as Wynne, Singer, Lidz, and Bowen began to ask about the interaction between the identified schizophrenic patient and his family. The model adopted led them to ask such questions.

Step 2 in the process was the building of theory. Theory begins with an observable fact, and then one asks questions like "I wonder what would happen if I made the assumption that the patterns of communication between an identified schizophrenic patient and his family were notably different from those found in other families." Such an assumption is called a *hypothesis* or a *premise*.

Step 3 in the process is testing our hypothesis. This means devising tests which will lead the investigator to either confirm or deny his premise on the basis of the data he has collected.(1)

The acceptance of the conclusion is what we mean by theory building. The researcher goes from one conclusion to another and in the course of time puts together a number of conclusions as acceptable.

If we return to our original questions, a nuance must be introduced. The questions centered on who was right and who was wrong, but in our explanation of theory we refrained from using the words "right" and "wrong." In theory building, one is trying to account for observable facts so that more accurately the words should be "good" or "bad" rather than "right" or "wrong." The question to be asked is not "Who is right or wrong?" but "Whose theory most fully accounts for the facts in a given case?" Whose explanation is most logical? Above all the pragmatic question of "Whose theory gives the best results?" must be asked.

Looking again at Figure 1 in the Introduction to Part II gives us a visual glance at various approaches to family therapy. Instead of asking "Which one is true?" we now ask "Which model is most in conformity to the observable phenomena?" We should ask: "Whose conceptual scheme gives the best account of the facts?"

Flowing from the pragmatic nature of theory, the first question to be raised is: "What does a theory do?" First, and most importantly, it leads to a collection of empirical connections which previously had not been observed. It gives us, therefore, new knowledge.

Second, a good theory not only yields knowledge but does so in a systematic way. This second characteristic is called *heuristic*. This means that one discovery leads to another, one insight leads to another, because the theory puts together a number of previously unrelated facts. The theory does not come along and say, after the fact, why a particular thing occurred, but on the contrary it is the cause of the discovery.

A third function of theory and related to point two is that it shows the observer where to look for data that might prove to be of value. This is nicely illustrated in communication theory. For example, as we have seen, Haley concentrates on the power aspects of communication. Amid the welter of material in a family session, both verbal and nonverbal, Haley says that "therapeutic paydirt" is to be found in observing the power maneuvers of the family. One may argue with the clinical approach he takes but it is consistent with his theoretical conceptions.

It is my contention that the major theorists in family therapy all have underlying theories of the family. The three questions put forth as critical issues were designed to get at this underlying theory. How one deals therapeutically with a family will be determined by his concept of the family.

The first question referred to the nature of the family to get at the "what" issue. The second question concerned the nature of change. Change can be, and is often, used with a variety of meanings. For one therapist it could mean a lessening of family conflict; improved communications, for another; or a more clearly delineated sense of autonomy and self-differentiation, for a third. This is one of the critical issues because therapy by definition means change. Granting this premise one must then describe what he considers to be change. Is it behavior, or must it be insight to merit the name of change? The answer is found in one's theoretical understanding of change. The issue here is how does one know a change has taken place.

The third question concerned the outcome of family therapy. This was associated with question two but differed from it in that it implied the agent or agency by whom or by which the change would take place. More simply: "Who would produce the desired change?"

The three questions asked in the critical issues were: "What is a family?" "How does it change?" and "Who effects that change?" The answers to these are tied up with the theoretical constructs of each theorist. These questions and answers illustrate again the role of theory. What one does as a therapist is tied to his conception of what a family should be and how it can change.

Although at present the theories in the field of family therapy are all inadequate in some respects, this does not mean that theory can be abandoned. For whenever two or more people meet and one is regarded as a therapist, then some concepts and assumptions, at least some implicit ones, are operating in the relationship. An axiom could be formulated which states that "In a therapeutic relationship one cannot not have theoretical concepts about what is or should be happening." To explore the roots of family therapy necessarily means getting into the abstract areas of theory and hypotheses. Consequently, the concrete and exciting arena of therapy, where the action is, can only be understood if the theoretical underpinnings are fully grasped.

Investigators have often observed that the therapist's own system of thinking and acting has an enormous impact on the client. The subtle influence of the therapist cannot be overlooked in any analysis of the therapeutic process.(2) The role of the therapist as participant observer is critical in individual, group, or family therapy, as Harry Stack Sullivan observed long ago.

TYPE OF MODEL

We are arguing from these facts that the initial way one puts the world together is crucial in all other structures. The basic outlook will color all significant processes. The starting point is the place of fundamental choice and option. Ackerman notes:

The history of science repeatedly demonstrates that a new method of observation alters our view of the problem; it produces a need for a new set of concepts concerning the nature of the phenomenon under study.(3)

Ackerman offers some insight into the nature of theory and its function. Relating this to family therapy the GAP report sees family theory as combining personality dynamics and multipersonal system dynamics.(4) All would agree with this assessment of theory. However, the critical question in the field seems to be the possibility of putting the two together.

Some of the people who opt for a system concept have come out strongly against any combination. As noted earlier, Haley, in particular, sees the two as discontinuous.(5) Similarly, Richard Armstrong, after a critical comparison of psychodynamics and a system approach seems to agree that the two are not compatible.(6)

A paradigm is a model, a way of conceiving reality and one cannot casually take concepts from one framework and transfer them into another. The issue then is not just peripheral but essential. Proponents of the system approach would argue that another kind of model, other than its own, is merely an application of individual dynamics to an interpersonal situation and does not give an adequate account of reality. On the other hand, a criticism of the system approach is that it is too mechanistic and oversimplifies a complex reality.

The theoretical issue can be represented in a diagram (Fig. 4) which illustrates the wide variety in thinking and in practice among therapists.(7) Again the diagram highlights, in a graphic way, how theoretical conceptions of a family and the role of the therapist are interrelated.

Fig. 4.   Analytic and systems interaction.

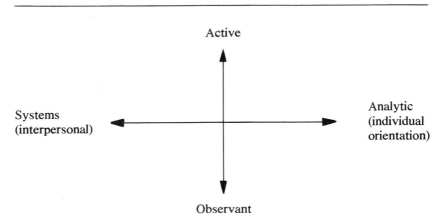

In summarizing the process of thinking in the field Ackerman says: "We have gone from a bioanalytic model to a psychosocial model to a systems model."(8) Depending on the lens we look through, we will see different things. The theoretical model used is crucial in the kinds of results obtained.

With these few observations in mind regarding theory building, we can now look at the similarities and the differences of our major theorists in a more enlightened way. How each of them view the nature of the family, the outcome of therapy and the role of the therapist in that process will determine their attitudes to a number of other significant dimensions.

NOTES AND REFERENCES

1. Haley J: Family Experiments: A New Type of Experimentation, in Jackson D (ed): Communication, Family and Marriage. Palo Alto, Science & Behavior Books, 1968, pp 261–289

   The Rorschach protocols done by Margaret Singer at NIMH with Lyman Wynne, et al. also illustrate this step.
2. Ehrenwald J: Psychotherapy: Myth and Method. New York, Grune & Stratton, 1966

   Ehrenwald deals with this at length in Chapters 11 and 12, pp 105–132
3. Ackerman N: Family Interviewing: The Study Process, in Ackerman N, Lieb J, Pearce J (eds): Family Therapy in Transition. Boston, Little, Brown, 1970, p 3
4. Group for Advancement of Psychiatry. Field Fam Ther 7(78):565, 1970
5. Haley J: Strategies of Psychotherapy. New York, Grune & Stratton, 1963, p 152
6. Armstrong R: Two Concepts: Systems and Psychodynamics, Paradigms in Collision? In Bradt J, Moynihan C (eds): Systems Therapy. Washington, D.C. 1972 pp 25–42
7. This diagram was suggested by Dr. Henry U. Grunebaum, a clinical associate at the Harvard Medical School.
8. Ackerman N: The growing edge of family therapy. Address given at the 10th Ann Conf Fam Institute, New York, October 23, 1970

10

Similarities and Differences in Major Theorists

CRITICAL ISSUES

The central issue in family therapy focuses on the nature of the family. A therapist must have some idea of an answer to the question "What is a family?" or he could never make the judgment that it is in pain. The technique or style of any therapist will reflect his underlying concept of the nature of man and his goals. This gives direction to a therapist whatever his orientation.

Therefore, a Freudian who sees man as caught between the demands of the id and the superego works toward developing ego strength. His concept of man as caught or trapped leads him toward the goal of freeing him from these. This goal, in turn, determines the process used to achieve the goal, namely, the necessity of developing a transference neurosis.(1)

The goal of Freudian therapy is a reconstruction of the personality. The unconscious must be made conscious and the ego must replace the id. This is the bedrock on which Freud built his technique. The technique, therefore, is linked to the theory.(2)

If one, however, chooses another kind of model seeing man not so much as trapped by his nature but as striving for growth and development, then the therapeutic process will be different than Freud's.(3) Since the goal is not the unveiling of the unconscious, the techniques chosen will shy away from anything which would increase the client's fantasies and develop a transference neurosis.

Satir also will opt for a health model, but it will be different from that of a Rogerian in that the paradigm she chooses will be an interpersonal communication model and not an intrapsychic one. Self-esteem is her goal, but it is the result of interpersonal rather than intrapsychic forces as we have seen.

The answer to the questions we have posed will derive from the model chosen. Ackerman speaks of interlocking systems. He will maintain that one must hold on to all aspects of personality: individual, interpersonal, and social. We characterized Ackerman as a bridge between the old and the new. He tried to go beyond the intrapsychic but would not go all the way to the system model. Conceptually, this presents him with problems because it leads to certain inconsistencies. Because he has a both/and approach to this issue his concepts of the family, its function, and goals will be different from the other theorists. The remaining theorists accept the system model although each has his or her own interpretation of it.

What Is a Family?

Ackerman sees the family as having two goals: ensuring physical survival and building the essential humanness of man.(4) With these goals clearly stated, Ackerman has moved into the area of value questions, for one must ask what the essential humanness of man encompasses. Such a viewpoint is heavily weighted with cultural factors. The process of socialization will vary from one culture to another depending on societal needs. Such goals as separation of children from parents, and their movement away from the center of stage to a more peripheral place, are highly conditioned. Ackerman therefore is concerned about culture because of its relationship to the process of socialization.

The family then is the major unit in socialization and is crucial for a society if it is to endure. However, at the same time, these societal goals cannot be attained unless the parents can also fulfill their personal needs. There is an interchange between the needs of the parents and those of society. For Ackerman the family is the place where society reaches people and where persons find their needs fulfilled. To understand the interrelation of these aspects, one must look closely at the theoretical understanding of roles, and how well or poorly these roles are carried out.

For Jackson "The family is an interacting communications network. . . ."(5) The goals of the family are determined by the parents, each of whom brings his or her own ideas into the marriage. They struggle for a definition of the relationship and each strives to attain certain goals. However, Jackson is much less explicit than

Ackerman about the nature of these goals. He is more content to open up lines of communication in the family system than to analyze why this or that goal is chosen. A family is a place where needs get fulfilled. When these needs are not taken care of, pain is felt. The therapist looks at the system and points out where pain exists and helps the system members communicate about their plans and aspirations.

Haley, too, accepts the idea of the family as a system. It is controlled by a governing process which maintains the homeostatic balance of the system. The family is seen as the arena in which power struggles go on. Haley holds that in every relationship there is a struggle for control. Each person is striving for certain goals which he wants to determine.

Satir holds that the family is the place where the attainment of self-esteem takes place. Although culture plays a part she feels that goals are geared to growth and survival. What hinders these goals is not good and the therapist must point out such things to the family. Enhancing self-esteem is the task or function of the family.

Bowen sees the family as an emotional relational system which is both needed and feared. It is needed for growth and survival, but at the same time it is feared because it tends to envelope and swallow up the person. A person therefore must learn to use it but not be over-whelmed by it.

There is a common theme in our major theorists. First, they all see the family as crucial for survival. It is the place where one fulfills certain goals and needs. Second, the nature of the family, although conceptualized in different ways, is seen by all as interactional, that is, one cannot view any part of it without taking into account the other parts. Since Ackerman, however, does not accept the idea of the family as a system, preferring to call it an interactional unit, the description will be limited to this phase.

From a therapeutic standpoint this concept has many implications. If the family is an interactional unit, then it cannot be excluded if the identified patient is to be helped. Although this conclusion seems almost evident, the fact remains that the family only rarely is seen in treatment. This procedure comes from the insistence of the traditional therapeutic approach that pathology is found in the person and not in the interactional patterns of the family. Different models yield different conclusions. But family therapists, beginning with the hunch that there was a connection between the identified patient and his family, have established a causal connection between the two. The conclusion, then, that the family is at least an interactional unit in which all members influence each other is the fundamental base of family therapy.

Nevertheless, it is not acceptable to individually oriented therapists who would see the family perhaps as exacerbating a person's pathology but not causing it. How this theoretical difference is used in practice can be seen in the way in which an individually oriented clinician and a family therapist would view schizophrenia. The former would say the schizophrenic was a "victim," whereas the latter would maintain that he is just playing a role in the family interaction. Furthermore, a family therapist would probably insist that the schizophrenic was, in fact, the one holding the family together! Family therapists demonstrate the validity of this claim by pointing out that the symptoms in a family have a tendency to move from person to person. This shows that such symptoms are not the exclusive property of a "sick" member, but caused by the functioning of a "sick" family.

All family therapists would agree that pathology is to be attributed to the interactional unit, the family, and not just to a person. Other therapists would see the family as adding to the problems of a person but not causing them precisely because they do not see the family as an interactional unit which is causatively connected to a person's pathology.

What Should the Outcome of Family Therapy Be?

Obviously, the answer is tied to our first question on the nature of the family. For Ackerman there are two goals: dissolving the current conflict and promoting positive aspects of the personality.(6)

In line with his conceptual model, Jackson states that the outcome of family therapy should be a recognition of the rules by which the system operates, and the implication that if they are known, a change or adjustment in them can be made.[5 (p 178)] This is why we termed Jackson's communication approach as one of openness. The rules by which the system operates are for the most part hidden and the therapist becomes the one who opens up the avenues of communication within the system.

Haley likewise argues for change as the outcome of family therapy. Haley contends that any change will break up the existing interactional pattern and get the system operating in a new manner. The family senses and feels its pain but can do nothing about it except demonstrate symptomatic behavior. It wants to change but is unable to do so.

Satir states clearly the expected outcomes of therapy: a person's understanding of himself and his ability to report this to significant others; the uniqueness of each person in the family recognized; and this uniqueness or difference used for growth. She too opts for change but is explicit about the kind of change. Apparently, some kind of change is not enough, but it must be a change oriented toward personal growth and development.

Bowen's outcome also is clear. The differentiation of the self from the family ego mass is the central goal of therapy. Bowen is more explicit than some other theorists in that he talks about ultimately being able to respond to the system instead of reacting to it.

Family theorists agree that the outcome of family therapy must be change in the family interactional pattern. But the change of which they speak is essentially a behavioral one. This means the interactional patterns of the family must change, and the members relate in new and different ways. This property is distinctive of family therapy, although not unique to it. The family therapist theorizes that if the interactional patterns change, then necessarily the individual members will change.

Again, a traditional therapist would not consider this change an "in-depth" one, but only a shift of symptoms. Family therapists, however, would insist that such a change was an "in-depth" one since their approach is not just supportive or one of counseling.(7)

Haley would criticize traditional therapy as being mostly an intellectual exercise that does not get at change in family interaction. On the other hand, he would insist that family therapy really does produce change which is lasting because it is behavioral.

There is then another area of agreement among family therapists. All would maintain that change in the interaction of the family is essential. The change they envision is behavioral, that is, people beginning to act in new ways toward each other. Such a change, moreover, is an "in-depth" one. Perhaps, Haley best stated the difference between individual therapy and family therapy in our interview: "In individual therapy you are supposed to change one's feelings and then behavior supposedly will change. In family therapy we change behavior and then feelings necessarily change as a result." Behavioral change, therefore, is the prime goal of family therapy.

How Does a Family Change?

Ackerman feels that a family changes when it comes into contact with an empathic therapist who helps it deal with its contagion of doubt, despair, and pain. Having developed a relationship, the therapist checks out a variety of family functions and begins to locate some areas of disturbance.   It learns to relate in new and more meaningful ways. [4 (p 296–303)]

Jackson attempts to disturb the family system rather than just pointing out problems. Also the technique of prescribing the symptom is frequently used. These devices upset the existing homeostatic balance, and force the family to establish a new equilibrium.

Haley states that by the use of paradox the therapist forces the family to change. It is an illustration of who controls the system, of who is in power. By taking control, the therapist upsets the balance of power in the system and literally moves it in another direction. Feelings are not the essential area of concern but power relations are.

Satir states that the therapist must become a model of communication. The therapist demonstrates in action what it means to communicate clearly so that one achieves clear, accurate, and meaningful communication among all family members. He learns the rules of the system and helps the family change them.

Bowen sees the role of the therapist as one who helps people detriangulate themselves out of the family system. By remaining emotionally detached from the system, the therapist forces the person to deal with his system and to differentiate himself out of it.

Obviously, the techniques used by each of our therapists are different. However, there is a similarity or common base. The therapist is an educator and a model. One may be warm and empathic such as Satir, or one may use a more detached approach such as Bowen. However, in either case, the family is being educated, that is, behavior is being modified. The family is learning new ways of interacting.

The primary role of the therapist in family theory is one of teacher. In individual therapy, on the one hand, traditionally, the therapist has been a blank wall or an empathic participant. The analyst, as noted, remains passive and detached and wants to create a transference neurosis. He makes a special effort to remain aloof so that he might better become an object of fantasy. He is more passive than active. A follower of Carl Rogers, although more active, will still shun the role of teacher. He aims at helping the client come to a deeper acceptance of himself. He does not, at least consciously, teach the client how to behave.

In group therapy on the other hand, the agent of change is not the therapist but the group. The therapist's role is to enable the group to function more smoothly. At times he is a facilitator for the group but not a teacher strictly speaking. His main function is to build group maintenance. His role is limited to either being an expert or a participant observer.(8) In either individual or group therapy he is not a teacher strictly speaking.

The role of the therapist then in family therapy is somewhat unique. Unlike the therapist engaged in individual therapy or the group therapist, the family therapist functions as a teacher. Specifically, he teaches new and more satisfying ways of relating. He is not an analyst, nor an empathizer, nor a facilitator. Primarily he is a teacher. Again, Haley has said this well, "Whether a patient encounters a therapist alone or in company with his family, he finds himself involved in a relationship which educates him by teaching him new tactics and providing a model for new behavior."(9)

Having seen the common roots of family therapy, by studying the answers given to the critical issues, we can now look at the specific differences among family therapists. For example, what are the similarities, if any, between Bowen and Satir? Or, in what way do the so-called communication theorists disagree?

How do theorists get from their concepts to techniques? How do they operationalize conceptual ideas? What are the procedures by which the theoretical concepts concerning the nature of the family, the goals of therapy, and the role of the therapist get spelled out in practice? In other words, what is the relation between theory and practice?

"Between the conceptual framework or theory of family therapy and the technique of its practices lies a middle group of operational premises that are either explicitly discussed among therapists or implicit in their work."(10)

The relation can be illustrated by a diagram (Fig. 5) which illustrates the notion that there is nothing so practical as a good theory. Our goal is to tease out some of the implications of a theorist's basic concepts.

Fig. 5.   The relation of theory to practice

Conceptual theory	Operational premises	Techniques

COMPARISON OF SPECIFIC DIMENSIONS

To watch a videotape of a therapy session by one of our five theorists is to see the basic concepts we have been emphasizing turned into action. The material picked up, the manner in which this is done and the direction of the session, all flow from some underlying premises regarding the family and its interaction.

Satir charms a family or becomes like a concerned relative because she wants to enter into the family system to find out what is causing pain and then move toward making the kind of change that can alleviate the pain. Bowen, on the other hand, remains aloof and almost withdrawn in order not to get caught in the family system. These attitudes are the result of previous decisions they have made regarding the nature of the role of the therapist in family therapy.

At every moment in the therapeutic encounter choices are being made by the therapist as feelings are being expressed, values articulated, and appeals made to the therapist. Amid this welter, the therapist ought to know what to choose and where to go with the interaction. For example, should one move towards the feelings being expressed or towards the cognitive aspects? Some direction must be chosen. To make the mechanics or the process of family therapy more meaningful, we have selected eight dimensions which are important factors in family therapy. We have rated our theorists as high (if the dimension is emphasized), medium (if it is considered but not of primary importance), or low (if the dimension is deemphasized).

This approach helps us see concretely the similarities and differences between theorists. It helps us understand more clearly the intricate relationship between theoretical concepts and their practical application. It enables us to tie together theory and practice. The categories chosen for examination are

1. History
2. Diagnosis
3. Affect
4. Learning
5. Values
6. Conscious versus unconscious
7. Transference
8. Therapist as model or teacher

These dimensions are not the only ones of importance, but they are essential ones and are connected with our three critical questions on the nature of the family, the process of change, and the role of the therapist.

History, diagnosis, and affect are mentioned in the frequently cited GAP report as important dimensions in family therapy.(10) History is important because the therapist can choose to look back, look ahead, or stay in the here and now. As noted earlier, the paradigm chosen will say much about this dimension.

Diagnosis, too, is a dimension which has to do with the kind of model chosen. The word "diagnosis" itself is used extensively in medicine and medical men are constantly searching for those elements which will allow them to make a differential diagnosis, that is, to be able to state that a given set of symptoms is related to a specific disease entity.

However, as we have seen several times, a health model does not make an analogy between a physical disease entity and an emotional dysfunction. Rather, symptoms are seen as roadblocks to personal growth and development and not as evidence of underlying pathology. Therefore, the dysfunctional person is not regarded as having some kind of emotional disease akin to a physical dysfunction but as one who must change the ways he or she has of interacting with others.

The question of diagnosis has relevancy in family therapy because the therapist must ask himself if it is necessary or even wise to look at the functioning in a family and call it by some name. Assuming that such a label is possible, one must then ask "But is it helpful?"

The question of affect is central in any kind of therapy. Human interaction always involves three dimensions: the feeling, the thinking, and the doing. The relationship of each to the other is of prime concern if one is to present an adequate answer to the question "What is change?" Does change involve only one of these areas or all three? Is there a hierarchy among them? Dimension three focuses on the area of feelings or affect. It requires each therapist to state the amount of importance he gives to the emotional component of human personality.

Learning and values, dimensions four and five, go together. All therapists across the entire spectrum from the most orthodox psychoanalytic follower to the latest faddist of some occult guru will insist that his procedures produce change. This of necessity involves a learning process. The orthodox analyst will insist that change is learning to listen to one's unconscious, whereas the faddist may suggest some arcane procedure, but in either case a learning process will be suggested. On this there is agreement, but the question of how overt a process this should be is debated among family therapists. Does the family have to know what is happening in order for it to change its interaction? Is it possible to learn new ways of interacting without consciously being aware of them? Furthermore, is learning to be restricted to cognitive areas alone, or does it include new behaviors as well?

Values refer to those goals determined by a family because of its culture and norms. Values are both personal and societal and result from an interaction between them. All therapy is value laden, but here it is a question of how openly are they to be discussed. Should values be made an issue in therapy, or not? Should a therapist bring conflicts concerning values into the open when they are causing problems or can he accomplish his therapeutic goals without doing this?

The issue of conscious versus unconscious has to do with the depth of the therapy. Many would insist that family therapy is not "depth therapy" because it does not focus on the unconscious. This position would maintain that only therapy which dealt with the unconscious would merit the name of depth therapy; all other approaches are superficial. This is because such therapists would label only characteriological change as therapy.

Several times in our study, the issue of transference has arisen. It is one of the perennial questions facing therapists. *Transference* refers to the collection of feelings, attitudes, and fantasies that a client has for his therapist, based not on their interpersonal contact but on the client's projections caused by early, largely unconscious relationships with significant others. At times, for example, the feelings, and attitudes will be warm and loving, but at other times these will be felt as rejecting and negative. The former type of transference is called *positive*; the latter, *negative*.

Transference like phenomena are encountered in therapy. Should they be encouraged, or not? If so, what kinds of transference, that is, positive or negative, or both?

The answer to this question will be related to the answer one gives to dimension six, conscious versus unconscious, since a prime way of getting at the unconscious is to encourage transference. If unconscious processes are important, then transference phenomena will be significantly highlighted in therapy.

Dimension eight looks at the therapist as model or teacher. One of the critical questions we asked had to do with the role of the therapist in the process of family change. The answer was that a characteristic of family therapy was that it featured the therapist in the role of teacher or model. However, the things one might teach and the extent of this role might be different for each therapist (Table 1).

We look at Ackerman first and then Bowen so that the communicational theorists can be seen together to understand better how an emphasis on cognition, power, or feeling leads to differences in practice among people with the same model.

The Role of History

Under this heading we want to discuss how important is the past to

Table 1
Dimensions

Theorist	1 *Hist*	2 *Dx*	3 *Affect*	4 *Learn.*	5 *Values*	6 *C vs ll*	7 *Tr.*	8 *model teacher*
Ackerman	M	H	H	H	H	M	M	H
Bowen	H	M	L	H	H	M	L	H
Jackson	M	M	L	H	H	M	L	H
Haley	L	L	M	H	M	L	L	H
Satir	H	L	H	H	M	L	L	H

a theorist. Ackerman is interested in history not in itself but for what it tells him about the current roles in a family. His locus is on relating to the family in an empathic way and helping it achieve its goals. The emphasis, therefore, is on the interpersonal, the here and now, more than on past history. History then is part of diagnosis but only a part.[4 (pp 138–147)]

Bowen places history high on the list. The goal of therapy is the differentiation of self from the undifferentiated family ego mass. Given this goal, history is clearly necessary to understand the family ego mass. Not only current history but history reaching into the more distant past is also considered.

Jackson stands somewhat in the middle. His interest can be summarized by the phrase "process over content." Jackson is interested in the repeated patterns in the family (process) since this tells him the kind of interaction going on in the family. History then becomes important only insofar as it illuminates the current interactional process.(11)

Haley shows little interest in the area of history. His focus is on power tactics. History, although obviously influential in a developmental sense, is not crucial in the here and now power interchange.

Satir, on the other hand, says: "I almost always start family therapy (or even marital therapy) with what I called a 'family life chronology' or history-taking process."(12) She has many reasons for doing so but two in particular stand out. The first is that history taking is a way of controlling the anxiety in a very disturbed family; and second, it helps her to make the point to the family that "things don't just happen" but are the result of certain decisions that people make in the course of their lives.

Diagnosis

Diagnosis traditionally means that the clinician is able to put a person or a family into a category of pathology. The concept of diagnosis is regarded as important by some, for example, Ackerman, and irrelevant by others, for example, Satir.

Ackerman writes: "A basic problem arises first in the area of diagnosis, for without adequate diagnosis there can hardly be adequate therapy."[4 (p 9)] Ackerman argues that without diagnosis there is no scientific approach to therapy. Everything becomes idiosyncratic because diagnosis and therapy go hand in hand.

Bowen takes a different point of view consonant with his overall thinking on family therapy. He opts for a movement away from the "sick" label to the concepts of dysfunction and behavior. Bowen observes that the family tends to project certain qualities on to a given member. The therapist must counter this by striving to move the family ego mass to a higher level of differentiation of self. Diagnosis then takes on a different meaning in his thinking because his conceptual model is not a medical one, but one which stresses functioning and dysfunctioning.

Jackson's central concept is family balance or homeostasis. He looks for clues which tell him where and to what extent the family is unbalanced. Diagnosis, therefore, plays a role in his thinking in terms of homeostatic balance, but not in the traditional way it has been used in therapy.

Diagnosis is not a particularly relevant concept for Haley. This is so because his model is also not medically oriented. Diagnosis has meaning primarily where the notions of health and sickness operate. Haley's model is one of communication, and he ties poor functioning, including schizophrenia, to confused or distorted communication.

Satir feels that diagnosis has two weaknesses: the first is that is helps the therapist more than the client, by allaying his fears of not knowing what is happening in the interaction; second, the categories do not help in treatment. They are not really of any value in approaching a given family. (personal communication)

For example, if family A is diagnosed in a particular way this does not mean that we will use technique A or B in that case because of specific factors. At the Family Institute Satir said: "Family diagnosis does not have the practical value of physical, medical diagnoses where a specific diagnosis requires a specific treatment." (Dec. 1, 1970)

The Role of Affect

How important is affect or feeling in family therapy? For Ackerman it is most necessary. The therapist acts as a model and so uses his emotions to touch the family. Ackerman writes: "To achieve access in depth, the therapist uses as an instrument his own being, his own emotions as he experiences them. The emotions stirred in a therapist facing a family group are diagnostic, provided that the therapist can correctly read his own emotions."[7 (p 110)] The instrument used for diagnosis and treatment is the emotions experienced by the therapist in his interaction with the family. Emotion then is the bridge between theory and practice.

Bowen has moved away from the feeling level to a more intellectual one. Knowledge and not feeling is fundamental in his system. He now works on helping people separate out their fantasy, feeling, and thinking systems. Consequently, Bowen does not stress the use of the emotional either by the therapist or by the clients.

The communication theorists seem to split into medium, low, and high on affect. Haley sees therapy as a struggle for control between the therapist and the client and so interprets affect in terms of what it says about who controls the relationship at any given moment. As a quality in itself therefore, he rates it medium because it is used in terms of something else.

Jackson takes affect into account but in a context of how others respond to it, in terms of family interaction. He uses affect but not so much in an empathic way, as Ackerman would, as much as a guide to the interactional process in the family.

For example, when asked if he has anything against people showing emotion, Jackson answers: "No, but I usually will comment on it if nobody else does." The interviewer remarks: "It's interesting that you bring up the weeping not in terms of those who are weeping, but in terms of the audience for it."[11 (pp 198–199)]

Jackson observes he is " . . . less concerned with the patient's personal feelings than I used to be."(13) Later on he admits he "ignores feelings" because " . . . feelings are so difficult to measure."[13 (p 108)]

Satir is high on affect. This is tied into her basic concept of growth. A fundamental part of this process is affect. "Growth therapy is based on the premise that people can be taught to be congruent, to speak directly and clearly, and to communicate their feelings, thoughts, and desires accurately in order to be able to deal with what is."[12 (p 182)] Satir is a communication theorist but her primary concern, especially in more recent times, has been the correct perception and communication of feeling above all else.

The Role of Learning

In all therapies, of whatever kind, the role of learning is a central dimension. However, it is approached in different ways by our theorists.

Ackerman stresses the clinical fact that one of the frequently occurring problems in family therapy is the competitiveness between husband and wife, in which each seeks to get the better of the other.[7 (p 113)] A therapeutic goal in these cases is to get the couple to realize that their needs are complementary and not contrary. How this is accomplished is illustrated by Ackerman at length.[7 (p 116–162)] His orientation here is fundamentally an appeal to reason. His approach is not only rational, of course, but cognitive learning, new ways of thinking are stressed.

Learning too is high in Bowen's thinking. The therapist tries to teach the family how it operates so that the family itself might become system experts. The process by which this is accomplished could be described as a suppression of old ways of looking at the family and the learning of new ways. Learning in Bowen's system is quite conscious and deliberate.

By contrast Jackson is not interested in the conscious process of learning but in behavior modification. "Prescribing the symptom is more likely to produce insight than telling people how the mind works."[11 (p 227)] This statement of Jackson is typical of both Jackson and Haley. Their approaches are all geared towards behavior modification. However, the means used are more indirect than those of Ackerman or Bowen. The family does not have to have "insight" into its dynamics but must change its behavior.

Haley ranks behavior modification as a major concern. In line with his central concept of control, Haley sees learning modification as the result of tactical maneuvers. Relationships are changed by reason of requests, commands, or suggestions that another do, say, think, or feel something different. These maneuvers, however, need not be conscious. Insight is in no way a goal.

Satir emphasizes learning. As mentioned earlier, the basic idea behind the family life chronology was to get people to see that things just do not happen but have a history. Families in trouble have a sense of defeat and despair, and she works hard initially to get them to overcome their defeatist attitude. The message communicated is that things can get better. The learning process is immediate since Satir recognizes differences in people as normal and points this out from the beginning of therapy.

Learning then plays a key role for all our therapists. However, Ackerman, Bowen, and Satir use more conscious awareness than do

Jackson and Haley. These latter theorists are more inclined to be manipulative in trying to change the behavioral interaction of families.

The Question of Values

"A clear and specific definition of the concept of values is fundamental to the question of healing and cure," states Ackerman.[7 (p 46)] He then asks the question: "Does the problem of values belong to the question of psychotherapeutic cure, or doesn't it? I believe firmly that it does.''[7 (p 49)]

Again one's theoretical model will determine the answer to this question. For example, Bowen's goal of differentiation of self from the family ego mass is a very definite value judgment. It is his guiding concept. One might say that Bowen's therapeutic approach is to teach this goal. Therefore, he clearly teaches a value system.

Jackson and Haley are less clear about values. Conceptually, communication is seen as the central issue. Of course we are talking about communication in the widest sense of behavior. In addition, a primary goal is helping people communicate clearly what they think and feel. Nevertheless, the what question, that is, the messages or values communicated seem of less importance to Haley and Jackson. To put it another way: the value question is present and is grist for the therapeutic mill, but these theorists would not necessarily raise the question of values whereas Ackerman would feel this as a necessity.

Haley, however, in our interview admitted that everything the therapist says or does involves value judgments. They are always present, but he does not feel they have to be made explicit, unless this becomes an issue in the treatment process.

Satir has very basic beliefs about human nature. She openly shares these with her families. It seems that one could say that, although not as insistent as Ackerman or Bowen, she is more inclined to deal with them than Jackson or Haley.

Conscious versus Unconscious

One criticism that has been levelled at family therapists is that the mode of treatment is superficial since the unconscious remains untapped. Ackerman feels such criticism is unfair and insists that there are depth experiences in families which are like those found in individual treatment, although he will admit adequate descriptive language does not exist at present.[7 (pp 108–110)] Ackerman says the therapist in dealing with families can go into this material as deeply as he feels is necessary. Unconscious factors are present and operative by way of shared currents of conflict, feeling and fantasy among family members and may have to become part of the therapeutic process.

Bowen, as noted earlier, is much less interested in the unconscious than he once was. With his strong emphasis on history and learning, one can easily see why this is so. The unconscious then is part of an individual member's and a family's history but it is not given a special place.

For Jackson and Haley this question is related to that of transference which deals with unconscious processes. The traditional notion of change is that of self-understanding. In addition, this kind of understanding can only be "deep" if there is transference present.(14) Analysts would consider any other change as superficial and not worthy of the name. Early attempts to shorten treatment, or lessen the development of the transference neurosis, were strongly criticized.

Jackson and Haley argue that such concepts are the result of traditional analytic prejudice. Moreover, the concepts of transference and analyzing the unconscious are greatly overrated. They maintain that change is dependent mainly on how one defines or describes change. Again, it is a question of which model is used conceptually.(15)

Satir recognizes the unconscious but is more concerned with the interpersonal than the intrapsychic. In a wide sense, the issue is not too relevant because of her growth model. The distinction between conscious and unconscious tends to blend together more easily in a growth model than in a health and sickness one.

The Importance of Transference

The relation of dimension six (conscious versus unconscious) and dimension seven (transference) is that the latter is largely the process by which the unconscious gets transmitted. In classical analytically oriented therapy, the medium of change was the transference neurosis. The therapist by his passivity encouraged the fantasy life of the client and so increased the transference and hastened the process.(16)

Ackerman argues that in therapy true healing only occurs when there is an exchange of emotion between therapist and client. In terms of family therapy, Ackerman maintains that there is a constant exchange of emotion between therapist and the family. Rather than ignoring this, he uses it constructively. Transference is not encouraged through passivity, but insofar as it exists in the therapeutic relationship, it is used.

Bowen insists that the therapist, if he is to be effective, must stay out of the system and this includes "staying out of the transference."(17) Emotional detachment is essential to avoid transference. The therapist has two roles: first, to be a catalyst for the family system, and second, to be the detached participant observer who interprets the family process.

As just noted, Jackson and Haley have written a paper in which their ideas on the unconscious and transference are treated. Again, it is a question of models. The authors point out that these concepts are intrapsychically oriented and in this framework have some cogency. However, in a system model, which is essentially a circular feedback model, the notions are somewhat anachronistic.

Haley, in another article, sharply criticizes the analytic approach seeing such therapy as a game of cat and mouse.(18) He insists that all therapy, directive as well as nondirective, is at heart a struggle for control of the relationship.

Jackson and Haley concentrate on the present, on the here and now. This follows from their insistence on the rules of exchange by which transactions take place. These rules, they imply, can change from day to day and " . . . could be different tomorrow, since the family is merely behaving adaptively in the social field they provide for one another in the present."(19)

Satir, in her growth model, believes that pathogeny is the result of the system and not of the person within it. Therefore, one must strive to change the system and not point a finger at the one who bears the symptoms. For her too transference is a notion belonging to another conceptual model and so is not directly dealt with in therapy.

The Therapist as Model or Teacher

This brings us to the role of the therapist. Like dimension four, learning, all would have to be rated as high in this category. All our theorists conceive the therapist as either a teacher or model or both.

Ackerman writes: "The therapist serves as an educator and a personifier of useful models of family health."[7 (p 101)] The therapist becomes the embodiment of those abstract qualities and values that are discussed in therapy. He is in touch with his own feelings and responds with warmth, honesty, and empathy to the family. Ultimately, the therapist's personality becomes the medium through which the helping intervention takes place. Ackerman likens him to a leader of a symphony who brings all the partial themes together harmoniously.(20) The therapist is both teacher and model.

For Bowen the therapist is like a coach. The analogy is most accurate. Since Bowen's goal is differentiation of self, it is best exemplified by one who has undergone the painful process himself. The therapist is a guide who leads the members of the family through the woods and into the clearing. He acts as a model of how one can relate to others in a meaningful way and yet not become overinvolved. The therapist is the one who responds and does not react. His control of self and inner freedom is a spur to others urging them toward the same possession of self. The therapist is the model par excellence.

Jackson views the therapist as the one who observes interactional patterns and then disturbs them. "If a family is stuck in a rigid pattern, the therapist should do something to break up that pattern," comments Jackson.[13 (p 102)] As noted earlier, he favors such techniques as relabeling and prescribing symptoms. He also tries to act in the role of model for the family by helping it understand shifts in the system and serving as a model who shows how such changes should be handled. This procedure is in harmony with Jackson's general feeling that the family therapist must be active if he is to break into and break up a pathological system. Instead of intellectualizing about change and its process, he demonstrates it by his own clinical behavior.

Haley summarizes the therapist patient relationship as teacher to pupil. This summary is in line with his analysis of how one knows a change has taken place in the family system, namely, by a change in the interactional pattern.

At the Family Institute, Satir cited the tasks the therapist must accomplish in family therapy. Yet all of these she summed up briefly saying, "You must share your world with the people you deal with." Satir holds that the therapist by being himself, by being in touch with his own feelings and thoughts, through a process of communication, can lead others to a new way of relating. The therapist is a model not so much consciously but as an embodiment of a number of qualities. One might say that, in Satir's thinking, the therapist is sufficiently integrated and the form becomes the content. The model is not an abstraction but the concrete person who shows others how one should communicate in a congruent and meaningful manner.

ANALYSIS OF SPECIFIC DIMENSIONS

In our comparison of the major theorists, just concluded, some striking similarities and differences can be noted. For example, within a system approach, there is a notable difference between Satir and

Haley on the importance of history. In this category Satir is closer to Ackerman than any of the other theorists.

Perhaps a comparison of Ackerman and Haley would be illustrative of how theoretical models influence practice. Ackerman's biopsychosocial model is an attempt to account for a number of observable factors. Consequently, in his work, all the dimensions cited have an importance for him. Haley, on the other hand, concentrates almost exclusively on the power dimension. Consequently, in his work, only learning and the therapist as teacher are greatly emphasized. His theoretical model gives him a point of view from which to do therapy. It tells him what to look for and comment on in the clinical situation.

Surely, the most striking features of our analysis are the dimensions of learning and the role of the therapist. All the theorists regard these factors as critical. In particular, the emphasis on the therapist as teacher is a departure from the traditional analytic approach. In analysis, the therapist remains passive and becomes the figure on whom projections are made. In family therapy, the therapist is active and not passive. Through his activity and intervention, the transference is lessened and the therapist becomes like the teacher who instructs by modeling and by example.

A final observation must be made. We have repeatedly observed that one sees according to the lens one uses. The use of model A or model B means that certain questions become relevant and others relatively irrelevant.

To use a psychoanalytic model, for example, is to take a certain stance in relation to the family. From this frame of reference, questions of transference are quite relevant. On the other hand, to use a system model, is to make such a question less significant because transference has meaning, more or less, within a given frame of reference.

Are our dimensions then only "straw men" designed to make differences exist where in fact they do not? No, because the dimensions chosen are present in some form in any kind of therapy. Certainly history, diagnosis, affect, and values cannot be ignored without a theory being incomplete. Moreover, learning and the role of the therapist have to be considered together since they interact. These too are necessary dimensions. Even the dimensions of conscious versus unconscious and transference, which seem to be tied to an analytic model, are present in some form in all therapy. Unless one totally denies the existence of factors beyond consciousness, then the question of the relationship of conscious to unconscious and transference must be asked. All our major theorists would recognize the reality of the unconscious and therefore must account for it in their thinking.

Transference, strictly speaking, belongs within an analytic frame of reference. However, there are transference-like phenomena operating in any therapeutic relationship. Jackson and Haley have answered this objection adequately:

> In this paper we will attempt to review the concept of transference from a somewhat different point of view. We will suggest a partially different way of looking at transference and the phenomena associated with it; a view that does not refute previous conceptions but simply adds a possible new dimension.[15 (p 115)]

Transference then is one of the dimensions that operates in therapy and must be taken into account. Therefore it is of major importance.

The eight dimensions chosen are not the only ones possible. However, they are among the more important. Moreover, they show quite clearly that there are similarities and differences among family therapists. They help us answer some questions raised at the beginning of our study, for example, "What is family therapy?" "What are the differences among therapists?" "Which differences are real and which are only apparent?" The analysis of the critical issues and their ramifications have answered these questions.

Having looked at the differences among theorists, a critique of the models used by family therapists will become clearer. In the light of our analysis of the major theorists, the role of their theoretical models in producing differences can now be grasped fully.

CRITIQUE OF MODELS

Our study of family therapy has unearthed a number of facts and put them into some kind of meaningful order. We now know what the similarities and differences are among theorists in the field, and as a result of this we can understand something of how these might be applied in practice. We have seen the connection between the theoretical aspects of family therapy and their use in practice. This brings us to a final step in our study, namely, an analysis of the models used since these lead a therapist to ask certain questions and to go in a particular direction.

A choice of a work model, for example, will lead to a series of dimensions different from those of a therapist who chooses a communicational model. The initial selection influences the final outcome. You may recall that the issues of true and false are not of concern in the choice of a model, but more appropriately one speaks of adequate and inadequate. Models are approximations of reality and not exact blueprints. Models are more or less inadequate and constantly must be revised and updated as new factors enter into prominence which must be accounted for in the overall picture.

Therefore, each model will have certain strengths and certain weaknesses. It will give a good account in one area and a poorer one in another. Models are inadequate, but necessary, if progress is to be made in family therapy.

We are now able to look at the models chosen and see their strengths and their limitations. It should be evident that a goal of family therapy must be to continue model building for without it the field quickly yields to chaos. A lack of systematic research, a paucity of conceptual models, and a general disregard for theory has grieviously wounded the encounter movement. Since it proliferated without a solid foundation, it grew out of control. Without adequate conceptualization as a base, practice did not have a direction to follow as "Do your own thing" became a slogan. But doing one's own thing is not always helpful and indeed can be destructive to self or others. Family therapy in its brief history has so far managed to avoid the pitfall of allowing practice without theory. One of my strong feelings and a goal of this book is to present family therapy as the result of the interplay of theory and practice. Our clinicians' contention is that the field has grown and developed because its thinkers did not sit in ivory towers and theorize nor did they ignore the demands of theory in their practice. The student of the field then must have an understanding and appreciation of both dimensions even though this work is concerned primarily with theory.

Among the major theorists two models are used: a biopsychosocial model by Ackerman and a system model by the others. Ackerman sees personality as the result of interacting forces of biology, psychology, and sociology. He insists that all three must be reckoned with in any answer to the question "What is man?" The other theorists choose a system model because they are less concerned with individual factors in the development of personality and more concerned with the impact of systems, especially the family system.

A Biopsychosocial Model

Ackerman was both a clinician and a theoretician. However, he identified primarily with the former. "I am a clinician first and then a theorizer," said Ackerman in our interview on January 5, 1971, although he felt both were necessary to evolve a valid concept of family process. As stated earlier, Ackerman felt that it was too soon in the history of family therapy to talk about a system concept as an adequate explanation of what goes on in family process. As a result, he talked about a set of hypotheses involving the individual member, the family, and the social milieu. This is a more awkward way of conceptualizing family process than a system concept, but the only one he had found adequate up to time of his death.

More specifically Ackerman focused on the concept of role and role function in the family. He maintained that role necessarily involves all three levels: the individual, the family, and the social. As we have seen, he conceptualized the family as a unit which had a series of tasks to perform. These tasks depended on the ability of the members to fulfill certain roles in reciprocal ways. In the same interview, Ackerman stated that the functions of the family involve five areas:

1. The family as a survival and growth unit,
2. Affectional needs of the various members,
3. A balance between autonomy and dependency,
4. Social and sexual training,
5. Growth and development of each member including the parents.

Ackerman's goal was to get a definitive description of a family which would include these various functions. No model had been offered which accounted for these functions and so he preferred to remain with the concept of a family as a biopsychosocial unit. The term was apt because it incorporated the three areas of family functioning: the biological, the psychological, and the social. It was apt but not adequate since it was at best a descriptive definition and not a definitive statement.

In practice, Ackerman seemed also to follow his theoretical concepts. Celia Mitchell, after observing Ackerman work with a family, commented on his style in this way: "While it did not ignore the family system, its emphasis was more on the interrelationships that determine the system than on the system determined processes."(21) Her observation illustrates the interplay between theory and practice. In 1958, Ackerman stated that his purpose was " . . . to evolve a conceptual frame within which it is possible to define the relations between the emotional functioning of the individual and the psychosocial functioning of the family group."[4 (p 11)] Since then he revised his model many times in an effort to portray reality as he perceived it in practice and to refine the basic concepts. The process was still going on at the time of his death.

A System Model

Our other theorists use a system model approach to family therapy. It, too, has advantages and disadvantages.

A system approach sees each of the component parts as related to the other, that is, a change in one produces a change in all. Therefore, to produce a change in the system, it is not necessary to work with all parts of the system but one alone is sufficient. Murray Bowen, for example, tends to exclude the children from therapy. He works with the marital dyad. However, even in this situation, he picks out the stronger of the two and helps that one differentiate himself or herself out from the undifferentiated family ego mass. If he can change or move one of the partners, the other necessarily will have to change in response. Even one shift in balance in the family produces reverberations throughout the entire system.

A second advantage of the system approach is that it tends to take the pressure off the family "scapegoat." Frequently, families have decided certain roles for various members. There is, for example, the "bright" one, the "quiet" one, the "good" or "bad" one. These labels have a tendency to stick even though a person may change radically in the course of time. Consequently, when family therapy is requested, it is often a plea "to help us with the 'bad' one." A system approach mitigates this and shifts the focus from the "scapegoat" to the family. If this shift can be accomplished, a new balance in the family has to be made, since the current system cannot adequately account for the new way of looking at pathology.

The third advantage is connected with the second. The shift from the individual member to the family tends to lessen the "blame," and to take away some of the force of guilt. If the problem can be taken from the individual member and moved into the way the system operates, then no one person is to blame. The question of responsibility and its concomitant guilt tends to get softened in the shift from the victim to the system. This has a great advantage. The members of the system are able to handle the problem now because they are not held personally responsible for pathology. One might say this approach tends to "defuse the bomb." The system then can begin to work on some of the problems in a more adequate and realistic way.

However, the system approach has definite limitations. It is perhaps too neat, that is, too abstract. Granted that families operate within certain limits, nevertheless, these limits are quite extensive. Families will vary tremendously even within the same culture. If a system concept is an advance, then it should give the therapist a tool of differential diagnosis. It should provide him with an instrument that not only gives him different pictures of family process but leads him to use specific techniques for certain family problems. The fact, however, is that a system approach is sometimes not too helpful in concrete cases in the here and now.

To illustrate: if certain processes are going on within a family system, these should be found in all families of similar structure, regardless of cultural difference, but this, in fact, is not so. We call this a limitation because at present, system thinking has not reached a level of sophistication adequate to deal with different parameters.

A second weakness concerns the question of the sibling subsystem within the main family system. Such subsystems seem to be vastly different within families. For example, apparently, in many disadvantaged families the children are expected to assume surrogate parent roles as several observers have noted.(22) The sibling subsystem in such families simply is not the same as that found in more wealthy middle-class families. Evidently, at times it is more a question of wealth than of color. In any case, the structuring of the subsystem is not the same. The question to be asked then must be that given these differences between family subsystems, for example, the sibling subsystem, can one really use the concept of family system in any meaningful way, or must one speak of a system that applies to family A and another that applies to family B?

Again, I am highlighting a limitation in a system concept. This is not the same as saying it is not of value and should be discarded. Rather, it is a way of pointing out the direction in which research must go to present a more adequate model for the therapist.(22)

A third limitation has to do with general cultural differences. I will suggest later that a theory of family process must take account of cultural differences that exist if it is to be adequate. For the present, it is sufficient to state that a major limitation of a system approach is that it does not incorporate into its theory the cultural factors that exist between family A and family B. It would seem to maintain, parodying Gertrude Stein, that "A system is a system is a system." But is not this attitude begging the question, wherein one assumes as proved that which is to be proved?

There may be certain givens found in all families apart from socioeconomic or cultural factors. One could hardly argue with Satir's observation that people in families want and need the same things, such as self-worth, love, acceptance, and the freedom to be. However, one could argue that the manner, or way, in which these needs get articulated or fulfilled vary greatly from culture to culture. Moreover, what is love or acceptance in one culture is regarded as rejection in another, and overemotionalism in a third. One need only think of a comparison of a Puerto Rican family, an Irish family, and a Japanese family and their concepts of love, especially the way it is demonstrated in affection, to see the result of cultural factors.

Obviously, a system thinker would not deny nor negate these factors but so far the development of system thinking has not been able to devise ways of handling such nuances. There is a tendency, therefore, for system thinkers to create a Procrustean bed upon which clinical data get stretched to fit a theoretical model.

The model used by Jackson, Haley, and Satir is called a communicational model. It is given this name because it focuses on the patterns of communication which go on within the family system. Specifically, it is interested in the rules of the system, that is, those feelings, thoughts, and behaviors that are or are not acceptable in a particular family. The therapist must ferret out those rules, and depending on his approach to therapeutic change, either overtly or covertly, move the family towards new and less painful ways of relating.

There is one criticism often levelled at such an approach. It states that there is a tendency for communication people to neglect content for process. This means that the therapist is concerned more with unraveling the strands of the family interaction than with the kinds of rules that the families uses. The therapist is interested in developing clear and open communication, but the substance of what is communicated is often shunted aside. The family functioning and interaction, that is, the "how" is important, but the family values and norms, that is, the "why" is of equal importance.(23)

The criticism then is that pain in a family is the result not only of the way communication is carried on but of the values that are communicated. There is some validity to this observation for, at times, in practice one encounters a family in which the communication is clear and direct, and the message given and the messsage received are congruent, but the value system adhered to or the nature of the interaction, for example, symmetrical escalation, is leading the family system into an endless spiral of pain, scapegoating, and recrimination. Certainly one could argue that the problem of George and Martha in *Who's Afraid of Virginia Woolf?* is not their communication but their relationship of symmetrical escalation. This pattern would have to be disturbed, but in addition some of the values espoused would have to be discarded if any kind of real change were to be possible.

However, Donald Bloch, editor of *Family Process*, makes the cogent observation that " . . . there is often a big difference between what people do, what they say they do, and what they believe they do" (personal communication). Although Satir, for example, is numbered among the communication theorists, yet her focus in practice is to deal not only with the patterns of interaction but with those values which cause disturbance in the family system. Satir obviously would not be content to help people become more aware of their communication, without at the same time, working on the content of what is communicated. Self-worth is not the result of any kind of communication but rather of the things said to a person about his or her value and importance as a person. Theoretically, one can separate content from process, but practically it is a very difficult operation since content and form tend to go together.

These observations on the limitations of a system model, notably a communicational model, are to be put into a context, namely, the complexity of talking about a multiplicity of simultaneous interactions. The model has outstripped the language in that we can now look at such interactions, but we still do not have an adequate terminology to express accurately what is observed.

The system model has proved to be a step forward in the way family interaction is conceptualized. As noted earlier, models are not blueprints but approximations. As such, they will have gaps in their conceptualizations which is why they must constantly be revised and updated.

NOTES AND REFERENCES

1. The role of transference neurosis in psychoanalysis is debated, at times, hotly. For an overview of the matter one might consult Chessick R: How Psychotherapy Heals. New York, Science House, 1969, Chapter 5, Transference and transference neurosis, pp 37–53
2. Ellenberger H: The Discovery of the Unconscious. New York, Basic Books, 1970

   For a full treatment of Freud's understanding of the unconscious see Chapter 7, Sigmund Freud and psychoanalysis, pp 418–570
3. Such a model is presented by Carl Rogers. For further study see Rogers C: Client-Centered Therapy. Boston, Houghton-Mifflin, 1951, Chapter 11, A theory of personality and behavior, pp 481–533
4. Ackerman N: The Psychodynamics of Family Life. New York, Basic Books, 1958, p 18
5. Lederer W, Jackson D: The Mirages of Marriage. New York, Norton, 1968, p 14

6. Ackerman N: Family-focused therapy of schizophrenia, in Scher S, Davis H (eds): The Outpatient Treatment of Schizophrenia. New York, Grune & Stratton, 1960, p 164
7. Dr. Ackerman was insistent on the point that change in family therapy could be as deep as in any kind of therapy. For further explanation see Ackerman N: Treating the Troubled Family. New York, Basic Books, 1966, p 118
8. Yalom I: The Theory and Practice of Group Psychotherapy. New York, Basic Books, 1970

   For a complete discussion of this see Chapter 5, The role of the therapist: Basic considerations, pp 83–108
9. Haley J: Whither Family Therapy? in The Power Tactics of Jesus Christ. New York, Grossman, 1969, p 117
10. Group for the Advancement of Psychiatry. Field Fam Ther 7(78):581, 1970
11. Jackson D: The Eternal Triangle, in Haley J, Hoffman L (eds): Techniques of Family Therapy. New York, Basic Books, 1967, p 207 ff

    In this interview Jackson shows how he uses history in a therapeutic encounter
12. Satir V: Conjoint Family Therapy (ed 2). Palo Alto, Science & Behavior Books, 1967, p 112
13. Jackson D: Differences between "normal" and "abnormal" families, in Ackerman N, Beatman F, Sherman S (eds): Expanding Theory and Practice in Family Therapy. New York, Family Association of America, 1967, p 102
14. The question of transference is at the heart of psychoanalytic process. For a good treatment of it by a well-known analyst see:

    Greenson R: The Technique and Practice of Psychoanalysis. New York, International Universities Press, 1967

    Chapter 3 is an explanation of the transference process, pp 151–357
15. Jackson D, Haley J: Transference revisited, Jackson D (ed) in Therapy, Communication, and Change. Palo Alto, Science & Behavior Books, 1968 pp 115–127
16. Ackerman N: Transference and countertransference. Psychoanalysis 46:17–28, 1959

    Ackerman gives an interesting development of these notions.
17. Bowen M: The use of family theory, in Haley J (ed): Clinical Practice. New York, Grune & Stratton, 1971, p 164
18. Haley J: The art of psychoanalysis, in Strategies of Psychotherapy. New York, Grune & Stratton, 1963, pp 192–201
19. Ferber A, Beels C: Changing family behavior programs, in Ackerman N, Lieb J, Pearce J (eds): Family Therapy in Transition. Boston, Little, Brown, 1970, p 31

The authors disagree with Jackson and Haley feeling their view is oversimplified

20. Ackerman N: The Act of Family Therapy, in Ackerman N, Lieb J, Pearce J (eds): Family Therapy in Transition. Boston, Little, Brown, 1970, pp 24–25

21. Mitchell C: Problems and principles in family therapy, in Ackerman N, Beatman F, Sherman S (eds): Expanding Theory and Practice in Family Therapy, New York, Family Service Assoc., 1967, p 113

22. Two studies worth consulting on this issue are:

Pavenstedt E: A comparison of the child-rearing environment of upper-lower and very low-lower class families. Am J Orthopsychiatry 35:89–95, 1965

Minuchin S, Montalvo B, Guerney B Jr., Rosman B, Schumer F: Families of the Slums. New York, Basic Books, 1967

23. Crocco R: The introduction of family-systems concepts within four schools of a low-income urban community, in Bradt J, Moynihan C (eds): Systems Therapy. Washington, D.C., 1972 pp 139–152

The article describes the difficulties he had with other professionals in using such a model and the one success when it was accepted. It is obvious that part of the difficulty is that system people seem very threatening to others in the field and need to work more in preparing other professionals for their model.

24. Ard B: Communication theory in marriage counseling: a critique, in Ard B, Ard C (eds): The Handbook of Marriage Counseling. Palo Alto, Science and Behavior Books, 1969, pp 213–219

This chapter details one such criticism.

Summary of Part III

In Part III I have pulled together the various dimensions, presented in Part II, in which we examined in detail the concepts of our major theorists and the answers to specific questions regarding the family, the process of change, and the role of the therapist in that process.

In Chapter 9 we looked at the role of theory in family process seeing how theory and practice were interrelated in that the former led to certain ways of doing therapy, and the latter furnished theory with new material; the two needing to be wed to each other for continued growth.

In Chapter 10 we looked at eight dimensions of concern in family therapy. Two of them, learning and the role of the therapist as teacher or model, were rated of major importance by all our theorists. The conclusion from this was that learning new ways of interacting, especially new behaviors, and the didactic function of the therapist were distinctive features of family therapy. I also included a critique of the models used: a biopsychosocial one and a system model, detailing their relative strengths and weaknesses.

One must ask a final question regarding the issue of models. Which current model will prevail or will new models need to be developed? The answer to this must be found in the ongoing interaction of theory and practice. Ultimately that model will prevail which makes the best accounting of the data available (theory) and which is most useful clinically in dealing with families (practice).

The conclusion to this lengthy excursion into Part III of our study is to remind the reader that models are an indispensable part of any approach which is called scientific. This study shows that the critical questions in therapy have to do with the paradigm or lens one uses to conceptualize what happens in family process. The choice of focusing on the individual member or the system, or some combination of both, leads to the developing of models which further determine the parameters of therapy. The purpose of the book is to show the connection among paradigms, models, and practice from their beginnings in the mid fifties until the present.

It is now time to look at the here and now state of family therapy, its present condition, and to make some statements about the possible directions it might take in the next decade. Part IV deals with these issues.

Perhaps the best summary of what this book is about was made some time ago by Jackson and Haley when they wrote:

When one shifts from a focus on the individual to an interpersonal orientation, many problems in psychotherapy appear in a different light. This does not mean that one point of view is more true than the other; each is equally valid from the point where the observer stands. Individual psychology has built a solid foundation; interpersonal psychology is just beginning to be structured. The ultimate choice will reside in which approach is most consistent theoretically and most practical in application.(1)

REFERENCE

1. Jackson D, Haley J: Transference revisited, in Jackson D (ed): Therapy, Communication, and Change. Palo Alto, Science & Behavior Books, 1968, p 127

PART IV

Family Therapy Now and in the Future

11

Family Therapy Now

Our study of family therapy has brought us up to the present day. It is now time to look at some current issues in the field and to see what direction family therapy might follow. The major issue seems to be the relationship of an intrapsychic viewpoint to a system concept. Is it possible to reconcile the two, or is there any value in doing this?

The GAP report states: " . . . the possibility must be kept open that the shift from the individual to the family is discontinuous and that the effort to develop a middle group is nothing more than an attempt to hold to the familiar."(1) This statement follows a suggestion made that therapists who work with individual members might gain much from working with whole family units and recommending to those at the other end of the spectrum the values of history and past experience.

A question of prime concern then revolves around this issue of continuity versus discontinuity. In the light of what we have presented in this study, one must ask if a middle ground is feasible any longer. Two theorists who would feel that there is a possibility of bringing together seemingly disparate elements are James Framo and Ivan Boszormenyi-Nagy. However, both theorists would recast the conceptual models of the past to incorporate some new ways of thinking about family process.

TWO INTEGRATIONISTS

Framo calls his approach a transactional one which leans heavily on the notion of projective identification as applied to a family system.(2) Earlier I mentioned the concept of object-relations in discussing Satir. Framo, too, picks up this theme together with a new way of viewing transference.

Fairbairn relates the growth of the ego to a satisfying early experience with object-relations, in particular, the mother. If this initial relationship is good then the process of personality development can go forward. Thus, a bridge is created between the intrapsychic and the interpersonal since the unfolding of one is contingent on the other. Fairbairn would maintain that the need for a satisfying object-relationship is fundamental in man and not, as Freud held, instinctual gratification. A child by nature is whole but needs good object-relations if that integration and self-acceptance are to continue.(3)

As Framo looks at families he has the importance of object-relations in mind. He feels that when the behavior of the parents is interpreted by a child as rejection or desertion, and the child is unable to give up the external object, it internalizes this loved but hated parent in the inner world of self as an introject or a psychological representa-tive.[2 (pp 129–130)] In the course of time these split-off, object-relations become important as the person begins to force close relationships into fitting the internal role model.

Framo's way of thinking is similar to that of Henry Dicks but goes beyond it. Dicks sees these unconscious, object-related needs form a dyadic unit in which the partners use scapegoating and projection to fit or reject the split-off internal objects.(4) Framo attempts to widen this concept by including several generations of the family.

What Framo seems to be saying is that the introject of the parent is a critical issue in family therapy and one that is much neglected. We are again involved in the issue of transference and transference-distortion but this time with a refinement brought about by a system concept. The transference in question is not just of the persons in the family taken together, summatively, but of the transference of the family as a whole, as a system. Framo is trying to put together a basically intrapsychic concept, introjects, with a system concept, and he comes up with a hybrid. In addition, he maintains that his point of view is contained, in essence, in the thinking of Bowen and Brodey.[2 (pp 132–133)] One might say that Framo is only teasing out the implications in their theory.

Framo feels that one must hold on to both ends of the spectrum in family therapy since each has something to say. He adopts a both/and position. He concludes his fascinating article by pointing out that the intrapsychic and the transactional are not to be confused since they exist on different levels and are not reducible to each other.[2 (p 162)]

Boszormenyi-Nagy, too, is attempting to build bridges between the intrapsychic and the system concept in family theory. He is interested in how the unconscious needs of the parents are critical in understanding the relations between the child and his parents. He maintains that parents who have been deprived of their own parents through death or separation often see the child as a parental substitute. Such a relationship, of course, is not healthy because it does not allow the child the possibility of separating himself from his family. The child's dependency needs are met but in such a way that the family becomes locked together in a destructive manner. This type of interaction is found frequently when the marital relationship is not need satisfying. When these needs are found together with certain communicational patterns and role structure, a family system is set up which is mututally destructive for all.(5)

A similarity to Bowen's concepts of triangulation and the need for a three-generational viewpoint can be noted. However, Boszormenyi-Nagy, unlike Bowen, is concerned about introjects and object-relations. Family pathology is seen as " . . . a specialized multiperson organization of shared fantasies and complementary need gratification patterns, maintained for the purpose of handling past object loss experience."(6)

Again, it is a question of trying to relate introjects to a system theory. It is an attempt to hold on to both ends of the spectrum, seeing something of value in each.

Over the years, Boszormenyi-Nagy has tried to hold on to both ends in his thinking. A developing concept in that process is that of loyalty which he feels forms a bridge between the person and his system.(7) In his clinical work he notes the needs for individual growth and system growth simultaneously. One must be loyal to himself but also to his system and at the same time. His recent work has been an attempt to bring together the demands of self and system. This concept of loyalty has led to a rethinking of the role of transference in family therapy. No longer can the therapist be content with isolating the identified patient from his family and becoming a surrogate parent. When the concept of loyalty is introduced, the therapeutic relationship is changed. The therapist no longer asks how he can become the parental figure for the client so that he can grow up emotionally, but now he asks how he might be of assistance to the whole family through the patient. The therapist and the client form an alliance, they become a team, whose goal is to improve the family interaction.[7 (pp 90–91)]

Why is this shift in perspective necessary? Boszormenyi-Nagy answers that loyalty to self and to the family system are both required. It is not realistic to ask that a choice be made.

The concept of loyalty again introduces a theme of this book and of family therapy: "How can I be myself and yet relate to my family system?" One solution, of course, is to make a choice and to live with the pain of anger or of guilt. The other is to struggle with both elements and to work out a pattern which is need satisfying. Loyalty is one of the concepts which cuts across both individual and system boundaries and leads toward integration.

At the present time in family therapy, all theoreticians, of whatever school, are struggling with the issues of differentiation and integration. Apparently, the general consensus is that both processes are needed. A person must become himself, and must separate himself from his family, and establish his own identity. This is a move towards the recognition of the other dimension, the need for integration.

The need for integration has been caused by the radical changes in the concept of family that have prevailed over the past 10 years. Not only has the traditional structure of the family been challenged but the very concept of need for a family itself has been raised.(8) Whatever the outcome of this upheaval, it is clear that things will never be the same. The female liberation movement, to cite one factor, has produced changes in consciousness which have altered the patterns of family interaction.

There is no doubt that the need to be one's self, to establish an identity as a unique person, is going to be part of whatever structures are created. Yet, as the existence of communes shows, there is also a need to relate to others. For many these others are and will be the family system. The concept of loyalty is one attempt to bridge the changes in societal structures between the person and his family system.

Boszormenyi-Nagy's concern in 1962 was focused on what we call the process of differentiation. In 1974, it is focused more on that of integration with the concept of loyalty being the bridge between the two.

A STEP BEYOND COMMUNICATION

Andrew Ferber and Christian Beels state that the earlier writers in the field " . . . see communication as *between* two or more people in an interaction pattern, where the moves alternate as in a tennis game. We see the moves as prefigured and synchronous, as in a dance."(9) The shift from tennis to the dance is a subtle one but important. The focus moves from one of "Who does what to whom?" to one in which the central issue is "What is it they all do together?"[9 (p 31)]

Earlier we talked about the importance of family rules for the communication theorists. Their focus was on the here and now interactional patterns. They suggested that the rules were different in the past and could become different again in the future, probably with help from a therapeutic intervention. Jackson, in particular, believed that the therapist had a mission to seek and destroy the system by upsetting the established rules by which it operated.

Ferber and Beels think this approach does not take into account the depth of the relationships that go on in the family system. They suggest that interactional patterns are deeply ingrained and to an important degree unconscious. Consequently, it is not sufficient to look at just one type of behavior, but it is necessary to consider the entire relationship. One is reminded perhaps of Eric Berne's concept of life scripts in which early decisions, also unconscious, are made as to how one will conduct his or her life.(10)

Ferber and Beels pick up this notion of structured life-long interactional patterns and state that an in-depth analysis of such transactions are required for permanent change to take place. Decisions of how one person will interact with another, and how they will carry on the business of life together is seemingly rooted in biology and sociology as well as psychology. It is not enough to cut off a piece of the whole and to feel this is sufficient.

Their approach then is an attempt to go beyond a communicational framework and the kinds of behavior that characterize the family system into the deepest parts of that system, that is, into the life-long patterns of interaction. To do this successfully, the therapist must widen his vision and include previously excluded dimensions of the family system. He must try to get a picture of the whole pattern and not just a slice of it in the here and now.

NO COMPROMISE

While Framo and Boszormenyi-Nagy are attempting to relate concepts derived mainly from psychoanalysis such as transference and introjects (with nuances) to system theory, and Ferber and Beels are trying to move beyond a communicational viewpoint, Haley is saying that no compromise is possible since the frames of reference are totally different. In our interview, Haley related, for example, that the introduction of object-relations into family therapy is an attempt to placate the psychoanalytic community since the concept belongs to an intrapsychic approach.

His original goal was to develop typologies of families. He now thinks this is not of value and should be replaced by longitudinal studies of families over an extended period of time. Apparently, family life goes through stages, but the hard data supporting this impression is noticeably lacking. The task is a formidable one since the researcher is pressed to keep track of his families over such an extended period of time as is required for such an in-depth study.

Haley sees the future role of the family therapist as that of mediator. He said in our interview: "The therapist in the future will be concerned with the mobile interfaces of the culture." He means that his role will be to mediate between the generations, between the races, and between the economic stratas of society. This seems to be attributed, at least in part, to Haley's thinking about the changes in the concept of the family. You may recall that he maintained that history and not blood would be the determining factor in what constituted a family.

His viewpoint seems to be that the changes going on currently in society will produce permanent changes in the social fabric. New forms of living and relating will emerge, but these will be forms radically different from those we are used to. As these changes occur, the therapist will move into a wider role than the heretofore narrowly defined one of healer of the sick.

The precise form his intervention will take cannot be determined during this time of transition. It is important, therefore, that his role not be solidified and so swept away by the ongoing storm. Haley is saying that the past is dead and that it is useless to hold on to what is no longer viable, at least in therapy. To try to build bridges between what has been and what will be is, at best, an academic exercise and, at worst, destructive to the birth of new forms; and ultimately, in either case, an exercise in futility. The forms of the future are not clear, but some delineation even now is visible. Our time and energy ought to be directed toward that unforeseen future and not wasted looking over our shoulders at what has occurred and is no longer relevant.

In summary, we can say that Haley represents an extreme point of view that does not see continuity between the past and the future. New experiences give birth to new forms and in that process things of the past must be discarded.

To close this brief discussion of the present state of family therapy, let me point out some of the key points made regarding the relationship of theory to practice. Theory is concerned with explanations and interpretations of events and is centered on the issue of why. Practice is concerned with what is happening with events and experiences and with the issue of what. They are related but not identical.

The explanations of "the integrationists," Ferber and Beels, or Haley, is focused on theory, on the why of events. One must judge their models in two ways: first, how adequately they explain observable phenomena; second, how heuristic are the theories; that is, how much further knowledge can they generate. In the long run family therapy will follow the direction determined by the theory that is most fruitful. The value of any theory lies in its ability to generate new ideas and ways of thinking.

All the theories studied so far are inadequate in certain areas or dimensions. Some are too narrow, and others too broad. Some include everything and others exclude almost everything. The reader must now ask if it is possible to formulate a theory of the family that is adequate. The answer, unfortunately, must be no. However, it is my contention that there are certain elements that must be included in any theory that claims to be adequate. Although the theory does not exist today, there is an idea of those dimensions which must be included. In the final chapter, we will consider the question of what is required for an adequate conception of family process in 1974, that is, in the light of past history and the present stage of development, we can discern the shape of the future, albeit vaguely.

NOTES AND REFERENCES

1. Group for Advancement of Psychiatry. Field Fam Ther 7(78):604–605
2. Framo J: Symptoms from a family transactional viewpoint, in Ackerman N, Lieb J, Pearce J (eds): Family Therapy in Transition. New York, Springer, 1972, pp 125–171
3. There is some disagreement about the child being whole initially. Followers of Melanie Klein, for example, would maintain there is a dichotomy from birth for everyone because of the presence of the death instinct and the life instinct. Cf. Klein M: *The Psychoanalysis of Children.* London, Hogarth Press, 1932
4. Dicks H: Marital Tensions New York, Basic Books, 1967, p 69
5. Boszormenyi-Nagy I: The concept of schizophrenia from the perspective of family treatment. Fam Process 1:103–113, 1962

6. Boszormenyi-Nagy I: The concept of change in conjoint family therapy, in Friedman A (ed): Psychotherapy for the whole Family. New York, Springer, 1965, p 310
7. Boszormenyi-Nagy, Spark G: Invisible Loyalties. New York, Harper & Row, 1973, pp 37–52
8. Cooper D: The Death of the Family. New York, Pantheon Books, 1970

    The thesis of the book is that the nuclear family as we know it is dead and new forms of relationships must be created. Cooper, an associate of R. D. Laing, has been greatly influenced by his antibourgois thinking.
9. Ferber A, Beels C: Changing family behavior programs, in Ackerman N, Lieb J, Pearce J (eds): Family Therapy in Transition. Boston, Little, Brown, 1970, p 30
10. Berne E. The Games People Play, New York, Grove Press, 1964

12

The Future: An Ecological
Perspective

What can be said about family therapy and its future? Having looked at
its past and present, something needs to be added to the picture,
namely, a perspective on the future.

What is required for an adequate clinical theory? Apparently, in
any theory there are certain factors which cannot be ignored. The
elements here can be reduced to three general concerns: family
dynamics, cultural dimensions, and a search for the underlying
structure of systems. These three factors are necessary as minimal
requirements for any theory which claims to be adequate.(1)

The title of this final chapter is "An Ecological Perspective"
because it is concerned about the relationship between organisms and
their environment. Ecology deals with the interplay between the two
and determines their interdependency. No theory of the family today
can afford to neglect ecological dimensions. The weakness of the field
of family therapy in the past has been that too many theorists have
done precisely that; for example, they have not taken into account all
the significant elements involved and consequently have produced
theories which are stunted for lack of breadth, emphasizing only one
dimension at the expense of others equally important.

The first concern has to do with family dynamics. This refers to
the myriad interactions that go on in the family system among the
members themselves and their relationship to the wider social society
of neighborhood, school, and other pertinent social systems. Long
ago, Ackerman began to pinpoint this parameter when he spoke of

troubled families as having "interlocking pathologies."(2) He saw that one could not separate individual, family, and other social systems into neat compartments. He perceived the necessary interactions that went on between them. At the time it was not easy to see these dimensions and even harder to articulate them as the language of interaction hardly existed. Ackerman and others, as we have seen, began to create the language which could capture something of the reality of what was perceived.

Another weakness of the early studies in family process was that it was based on a largely schizophrenic population. Although generalizations were made to other kinds of people the samples were often small and conditioned by socioeconomic factors. It was necessary, therefore, to begin to look at some anthropological data to get a truer picture. One of the pioneers in this area was John Spiegel(3) who had a twofold interest: one in the function of role as a way of talking about the exchanges between various systems; and the other, cultural dimensions, especially the question of values. Spiegel writes: "I see the family in general as a system of reciprocal patterns and processes operating within a larger field of interpenetrating systems. Role and values are crucial in the workings of the system."[3 (p 201)]

Such a viewpoint is a step beyond the initial attempts to characterize family process since it specifically includes culture. Roles and values are culturally defined in that they grow out of a *gestalt* which includes religion and education as well as family, all interacting. It is clear, for example, that a family in Japan would be different from one in New York City, precisely because the roles in the family and the value system would be different. Even granting that the system might operate in a similar way, for example, made up of a series of interlocking triangles, one must ask if the cultural differences would not be critical in how one approaches the family.

Spiegel translates these notions into practice by presenting a long analysis of two Italian families, one labeled "well," and the other "sick."[3 (pp 201–309)] Although each family shares a common heritage, nevertheless, the ways that roles and values get spelled out in the two families are different with one path leading to health and the other to sickness.

In another article he talks about how the phenomena of transference and countertransference will operate in a therapeutic relationship depending on the religious orientation of the client and the therapist.(4) Surely today, a white therapist working with a black family must be aware of this difference as an important factor to be considered in any diagnostic plan.

Salvador Minuchin is one current family therapist who looks at cultural factors as important elements in the treatment process. In *Families of the Slums* he and his associates analyze in detail some of the cultural dimensions found in the black and Puerto Rican families that they studied.(5) Because of these, Minuchin states that some specific kinds of therapeutic maneuvers are necessary. Why? The roles and the values are different in different cultures. The therapist is seen in one way in one culture, and in another way in another. Recalling earlier observations on the relationship of feeling, thinking, and willing is helpful at this point. The emphasis given in treatment to cognitive dimensions, for example, will be measured in part by cultural factors. In a system that prizes highly an understanding of human dynamics, much time might be spent on a search for the whys of family interaction. For that kind of family might prize such a value and want some kind of understanding. A less intellectual and more active family, on the other hand, might want only some change in feelings and a lessening of the emotional contagion that seems to have it in its grip. A "why" approach would not be helpful because it would not be of value.

Surprisingly, little has been done with cultural factors in family therapy. Are all families to be approached in the same way, or not? If not, then why not? Are the differences in families in roles and value, both of which are often dissimilar, of critical importance, or not? Finally, if they are, does a knowledge of these differences lead family therapists to make specifically different interventions, or not? The area is open to research and sorely in need of it.

Gerald Zuk, too, has begun to make some suggestions in relation to the therapist and certain kinds of families.(6) He suggests, for instance, that the family therapist working with a lower-class black family is more in the role of "celebrant," as one who seals a process of change, than as one who induces change. He sees the therapist as an agent between the family and society. This is in line with his concept of the therapist as a go between.(7)

Although his thinking is still in a nascent state, it seems to be moving in a direction which sees the therapist as working at the interfaces of society, that is, at those points where one system impinges on another. This is in line with what we have termed an ecological perspective.

In his multiple family therapy approach, Peter Laqueur tries to deal with cultural differences by bringing together, at the same time, five or six families of different backgrounds. Using a general system theory, Laqueur trains his students to work at the interfaces between various systems with an emphasis on affective rather than cognitive boundaries.(8)

He describes the role of the therapist as a most delicate one in which he carries information across the boundaries between systems without rupturing them.(9) The emphasis here is on the ways in which information is received and processed by a person. Implicit in his concept is the notion that change in behavior is conditioned by a change in information.

Laqueur is combining a number of elements in his therapeutic approach: general system theory, an awareness of culture, the need for information, the role of learning in change, and the therapist as one who works at the interfaces and boundaries between various interactional systems. It is a rich blend of theory and practice constantly being refined and developed, and always aware of the changes going on in society and their effect on the family system.

The third factor required for an adequate theory and clinical view can be called *structural*. This refers to those who are working on an analysis of family systems trying to uncover their basic underpinnings. Most notably, Murray Bowen and his adherents constitute one of the groups which can be called structuralist in that they are concerned with this problem of what makes up a family system. The aforementioned *Systems Therapy* is a collection of papers articulating the theory, technique, and research of Bowenian thought.(10)

Minuchin, Haley, and their associates, in Philadelphia, also are concerned about family structure. In particular, they are concerned with developing tactics or strategies leading to effective family intervention. One of their most effective interventions is to deliberately induce a crisis in a family so that some kind of change is required by the family system to cope with the crisis.(11) Their experience seems to indicate that family homeostasis can only be broken up by strong interventions by a therapist or a therapeutic team. The added value in their approach is that many of their clients are disadvantaged so that cultural dimensions must be taken into account in any therapeutic maneuver.

One way of effectively getting at family structures that has been developed is that of "family sculpting" or "family sculpture."(12) Basically, each member of a family is asked to create a picture of his family as he sees it using space to indicate distance or intimacy and posture to indicate emotional states such as joy, sadness, indifference. It conveys, often dramatically, the difference that exists between the way one family member sees his family and the way another one views it. In addition, it shows graphically how feeling states are not attributable to intrapsychic forces alone but are the result of system interaction. Moreover, it has the added value of being of use with "well" families as much as with "sick" ones.(13) It has great potential for helping families avoid future problems by giving them a tool to use which is preventive as well as corrective.

Any clinical situation involves some combination of these parameters of family dynamics, culture, and family structure. Therefore, a clinical theory of family therapy must embrace all three if it is to be adequate.

Family therapy must have an ecological perspective if it is to make the kinds of intervention that are necessary to help families. A system theory sees the family as an open system amid other open systems. This means that the boundaries touch and are semipermeable, that is, capable of being penetrated. Exchanges of information are possible and with new learnings come new behaviors. Theorists have argued that the family system is not one which is closed and isolated but open to other systems. Therefore, family therapy cannot cut out these other systems which impinge on it. Cultural dimensions, too, modify a given family system by emphasizing certain roles and values and cannot be ignored. Finally, the basic structures of the family have to be investigated so that the similarities and differences, that is, those underlying human patterns that transcend cultural barriers and those nuances that are culturally conditioned can be separated. This is a formidable task.

What an ecological perspective gives is a more complete picture of what is going on in a particular situation. Within a framework of a system concept, it looks at the various systems and subsystems involved to get a total picture of what is happening. It then focuses precisely on the interfaces between these systems in the attempt to produce change.(14) It takes account of a multiplicity of data without emphasizing one aspect at the expense of another.

A clinical picture of a family then will involve a number of dimensions from various systems and subsystems. Such an approach is truly different because it refuses to separate and parcel out portions as if they did not interact. The model it presents is one which incorporates all the factors into a new *gestalt.* Therefore, a general system model is required as a skeleton for family therapy to be effective. However, the model must include cultural nuances and subsystem interactions if it is to give a true picture of family system.

In this chapter I have delineated the elements required for an adequate theory and clinical picture of family therapy in our time. No single model as yet exists which offers an adequate explanation of what goes on in family interaction. The goal of our time must be to work toward more adequate models and theories of family process. As in the past this will be an interactional process of theory and practice, the one feeding the other. In the final analysis, of course, no one model will be sufficient since new knowledge will always require new forms and will give birth to them. However, we in the field now have an idea of the general direction to follow if family therapy is to survive and become a viable therapeutic tool in the future.

SUMMARY

An Introduction to Family Therapy has presented an introduction to a complex field involving psychological dimensions, social factors, and general system theory. Family therapy is a field that has grown enormously in fewer than 20 years. It began with an insight that the pathological functioning of an identified patient might in some significant way be related to the family system to which he belonged. That beginning marked a shift from an exclusively intrapsychic approach to an interpersonal one. In time a system model was created to account for the multiplicity of ongoing interactions with the family which were simultaneous.

On the basis of family theory and practice in the last decade another question has arisen, namely, "In what way is the family, now conceptualized as a system, influenced by other systems in the culture?" This is the point of history of family therapy at the present. Today, the interaction is recognized but no model adequate to the reality has been developed. In lieu of this the family therapist must focus on the interfaces between systems.

We are at an interesting time in the history of family therapy because we now know something of importance, that is, a family system is greatly influenced by other systems, but we do not have a model that helps us develop this insight. What is needed is to work toward a model that will take account of system interaction in such a way that it will lead to the invention of therapeutic strategies capable of moving family systems. Within the context of a general system theory, family therapy must examine more closely that unique, interacting, open system called the family. The task of family therapy in this decade then will be to seek new ways of conceptualizing family process that take adequate cognizance of the world in which we live, and hopefully, to move towards therapeutic interventions of benefit to a troubled family system and bring, at least to this critical sector of society, some alleviation of pain.

NOTES AND REFERENCES

1. This chapter is the result of extended conversations with Dr. John Pearce, a noted theoretician and clinician of family therapy, whose support, encouragement, and friendship has been of incalculable benefit.

2. Ackerman N: Interlocking pathologies in family relationships, in Rado S, Daniels G (eds): Changing Concepts in Psychoanalytic Medicine. New York, Grune & Stratton, 1956, pp 135–150

3. Spiegel J: Transactions—The Interplay between Individual, Family and Society. New York, Science House, 1971

    As noted earlier, Ackerman felt Spiegel's concept of role had great clinical value.

4. Spiegel J: Some cultural aspects of transference and countertransference, in Masserman, J (ed): Science and Psychoanalysis, Individual and Familial Dynamics, vol. II. New York, Grune & Stratton, 1959, pp 160–182

5. Minuchin S, Montalvo B, Guerney B Jr, Rosman B, Schumer F: Therapeutic interventions, in Families of the Slums. New York, Basic Books, 1967, pp 244–297

6. Zuk G: Technique in family therapy. Address given at the annual convention of the Am Assoc Marriage and Fam Counselors, Palm Springs, Calif., Nov. 3, 1973

7. Zuk G: Family Therapy: To go-between process in family therapy, in A Triadic-Based Approach. New York, Behavioral Publications, 1971, pp 45–63

8. Laqueur P: Multiple family therapy: Questions and answers, in Bloch D (ed): Techniques of Family Therapy A Primer. New York, Grune & Stratton, 1973 pp 75–85

9. Laqueur P: General systems theory: A Tool for Understanding group therapy—theory and practice. Address given at the annual convention of the Am Group Psychiatr Assoc, Detroit, Michigan Feb. 8, 1973

10. Bradt J, Moynihan C (eds): Systems Therapy. Washington, D.C., Groome Child Guidance Clinic, 1972

11. Minuchin S, Barcai A: Therapeutically induced family crisis, in Masserman J (ed): Science and Psychoanalysis, vol. 14. New York, Grune & Stratton, 1969 pp 199–206

    For further reading on family structure see Minuchin S: Structural family therapy, in Caplan G (ed): American Handbook of Psychiatry, vol. 2. New York, Basic Books, 1974, pp 178–192

12. Duhl F, Kantor D, Duhl B: Learning, space, and action in family therapy: A primer of sculpture, in Bloch D (ed): Techniques of Family Therapy A Primer. New York, Grune & Stratton, 1973 pp 47–63

13. Papp P, Silverstein O, Carter E: Family sculpting in preventive work with "well families." Fam Process 12:197–212, 1973

14. For an illustration of an ecological perspective clearly illuminated by a
     case, see Auerswald E: Interdisciplinary versus ecological approach in
     progress, in Sager C, Kaplan H (eds): Family and Group Therapy. New
     York, Brunner/Mazel, 1972, pp 309–321

     Also Minuchin S: Family therapy: theory or technique? in Masserman J
     (ed): Science and Psychoanalysis, vol. 14. New York, Grune & Stratton,
     1969, pp 179–187, especially pp 186–187.

     Also Minuchin S: Structural Family Therapy, in Caplan G. (ed): American
     Handbook of Psychiatry, vol 2. New York, Basic Books, 1974, pp 178–
     192.

BIBLIOGRAPHY

Ackerman, Nathan. "Family-Focused Therapy of Schizophrenia." In the *Out-Patient Treatment of Schizophrenia.* S. Scher and H. Davis (eds). New York, Grune & Stratton, 1960

———. "Family Interviewing: The Study Process." In *Family Therapy in Transition.* N. Ackerman, J. Lieb, J. Pearce (eds). Boston, Little, Brown & Co., 1970

———. "Family Psychotherapy Today." *Family Process* 9: 123–127

———. "Interlocking Pathologies In Family Relationships," in *Changing Concepts in Psychoanalytic Medicine.* S. Rado, G. Daniels (eds). New York, Grune & Stratton, 1956

———. "Interpersonal Disturbances in the Family: Some Unresolved Problems in Psychotherapy." *Psychiatry* 17: 359–368

———. "Psychological Dynamics of the 'Familial Organism' in *The Family: A Focal Point in Health Education.* I. Galdston (ed). New York, International University Press, 1961

———. "Social Role and Total Personality." *Am J Orthopsychiatry.* 21 (1951), 1–18

———. "The Art of Family Therapy," in *Family Therapy in Transition.* N. Ackerman, J. Lieb, J. Pearce (eds). Boston, Little, Brown & Co., 1970

———. "The Future of Family Psychotherapy." In *Expanding Theory and Practice in Family Therapy.* N. Ackerman, F. Beatman, S. Sherman (eds). New York, Family Association of America, 1967

———. *The Psychodynamics of Family Life.* New York, Basic Books, 1958

———. "The Unity of the Family." *Archives of Pediatrics* 55 (1938): 51–62

———. "Transference and Countertransference." *Psychoanalysis* 46 (1969): 17–28

———. *Treating the Troubled Family.* New York, Basic Books, 1966

Adler, Alfred. *The Practice and Theory of Individual Psychology.* New York, Humanities Press, 1952

Albee, Edward. *Who's Afraid of Virginia Woolf?* New York, Pocket Books, 1964

Anonymous. "Towards the Differentiation of a Self in One's Own Family." In Family Interaction: A Dialogue Between Family Researchers and Family Therapists. J. Framo (ed). New York, Springer, 1972

Ard, Ben. "Communication Theory in Marriage Counseling: A Critique." In the *Handbook of Marriage Counseling.* B. Ard, C. Ard (eds). Palo Alto, Science and Behavior Books, 1969

Armstrong, Richard. "Two Con-

184

cepts: Systems and Psychodynamics, Paradigms in Collision?" In *Systems Therapy*. J. Bradt, C. Moynihan (eds). Washington, D.C., 1972

Auerswald, Edgar. "Interdisciplinary versus Ecological Approach." In Progress in *Family and Group Therapy*, C. Sager, H. Kaplan (eds). New York, Brunner/Mazel, 1972

Bateson, Gregory. *Steps To An Ecology Of Mind*. New York, Ballantine Books, 1972

Bateson, Gregory; Jackson, Don; Haley, Jay; and Weakland, John. "A Note on the Double Bind." *Communication, Family and Marriage*. Don Jackson (ed). Palo Alto, Science and Behavior Books, 1968

Bateson, Gregory; Jackson, Don; Haley, Jay; Weakland, John. "Toward a Theory of Schizophrenia in *Communication, Family and Marriage*. D. Jackson (ed). Palo Alto, Science and Behavior Books, 1968

Berne, Eric. *The Games People Play*. New York, Grove Press, 1964

Block, Donald; La Perriere, Kitty. "Techniques of Family Therapy: A Conceptual Framework." In *Techniques of Family Therapy A Primer*. D. Block (ed). New York, Grune & Stratton, 1973

Boszormenyi-Nagy, Ivan. "The Concept of Change in Conjoint Family Therapy." In *Psycho-therapy for the Whole Family*. A. Friedman (ed). New York, Springer Publishing Company, 1965

————. "The Concept of Schizophrenia from the Perspective of Family Treatment." *Family Process* I (1962): 103–113

Boszormenyi-Nagy, Ivan, and Spark, Geraldine. *Invisible Loyalties*. New York, Harper & Row, 1973

Bowen, Murray. "A Family Concept of Schizophrenia." In the *Etiology of Schizophrenia*. D. Jackson (ed). New York, Basic Books, 1960

————. "Family Psychotherapy." *Am J Orthopsychiatry* 31 (1961): 40–60

————. "Family Psychotherapy with Schizophrenia in the Hospital and in Private Practice." In *Intensive Family Therapy*. I. Boszormenyi-Nagy, J. Framo (eds). New York, Harper & Row, 1965

————. "Principles and Techniques of Multiple Family Therapy." In *Systems Therapy*. J. Bradt, C. Moynihan (eds). Washington, D.C. 1972

————. "The Use of Family Theory in Clinical Practice." In *Changing Families*, J. Haley (ed). New York, Grune & Stratton, 1971

Bowen, Murray; Dysinger, R; and Basamania, B. "The Role of the Father in the Family Environment of the Schizophrenic Patient." *Amer. J. of Psychiatry* 115 (1959): 1017–1020

Bradt, J, Moynihan, C. *Systems Therapy*. Washington, D.C., 1972

Brodey, Warren. "Some Family Operations and Schizophrenia." *Archives of Gen. Psychiatry,* I (1959): 379–402

Chessick, Richard. *How Psychotherapy Heals.* New York, Science House, 1969

Christensen, Oscar. "Family Counseling: An Adlerian Orientation." In *Proceedings of a Symposium on Family Counseling and Therapy.* G. Gazda (ed). Athens, Georgia, Univ. of Georgia—School of Education, 1971

Cooper, David. *The Death of the Family.* New York, Pantheon Books, 1970

Crocco, Richard. "The Introduction of Family-Systems Concepts Within Four Schools." In *Systems Therapy.* J. Bradt, C. Moynihan (eds). Washington, D.C., 1972

Dicks, Henry. *Marital Tensions.* New York, Basic Books, 1967

Duhl, Fred; Kantor, David; Duhl, Bunny. "Learning, Space, and Action in Family Therapy: A Primer of Sculpture." In *Techniques of Family Therapy A Primer,* D. Bloch (ed). New York, Grune & Stratton, 1973

Ehrenwald, Jan. *Psychotherapy Myth and Method.* New York, Grune and Stratton. 1966

———. *Neurosis in the Family.* New York, Harper & Row, 1960

Ellenberger, Henri. *The Discovery of the Unconscious.* New York, Basic Books, 1970

Erickson, Milton. *"Indirect Hypnotherapy of a Bedwetting Couple in Changing Families,* J. Haley (ed). New York, Grune & Stratton, 1971

Fairbairn, W.R.D. *"An Object-Relations Theory of Personality."* New York, Basic Books, 1954

Ferber, Andrew, and Beels, Christian. "Changing Family Behavior Programs." In *Family Therapy in Transition.* N. Ackerman, J. Lieb, J. Pearce (eds). Boston, Little, Brown & Company, 1970

Foley, Vincent. *"Conceptual Roots of Conjoint Family: A Comparative Analysis of Major Theorists."* Boston, Boston Univ. Unpublished Dissertation, 1971

Framo, James. Family Interaction: A Dialogue Between Family Researchers and Family Therapists. J. Framo (ed). New York, Springer Publishing Company, 1972

Framo, James. "Symptoms From a Family Transactional Viewpoint." In *Family Therapy in Transition.* N. Ackerman, J. Lieb, J. Pearce. (eds). Boston, Little, Brown and Company, 1970

Freud, Sigmund. "Analysis of Phobia in a Five-Year Old Boy." *The Complete Works of Sigmund Freud.* J. Strachey, London, Hogarth Press, 1964

Gray, William and Rizzo, Nicholas. "History and Development of General Systems Theory and Psychiatry." In *General Systems Theory and Psychiatry.* W. Gray, F. Duhl, N. Rizzo (eds). Boston, Little, Brown & Co., 1969

186

Greenburg, Dan. *How To Be a Jewish Mother.* Los Angeles, Price, Sloan and Stern, 1964

Greenson, Ralph. *"The Technique and Practice of Psychoanalysis.* New York, International Universities Press, 1967

Grotjahn, Martin. *Psychoanalysis and the Family Neurosis.* New York, W. W. Norton, 1960

Group for the Advancement of Psychiatry. *The Field of Family Therapy,* 7, n. 78. New York, 1970

Grunebaum, Henry, and Bryant, Charles. "The Theory and Practice of the Family Diagnostic. Part II. Theoretical Aspects and Resident Education." In *Family Structure, Dynamics and Therapy.* I. Cohen (ed). Washington, Psychiatric Research Reports of the APA, 1966

Haley, Jay. "Approaches to Family Therapy." In *Changing Families* J. Haley (ed). New York, Grune & Stratton, 1971

———. "A Review of the Family Therapy Field." In *Changing Families.* J. Haley (ed). New York, Grune & Stratton, 1971

———. "An Interactional Description of Schizophrenia." *Psychiatry* 22 (1959): 321–332

———. "Family Experiments: A New Type of Experimentation." In *Communication, Family and Marriage.* D. Jackson, (ed). Palo Alto, Science & Behavior Books, 1968

———. "Family Therapy: A Radical Change." In *Changing Families.* J. Haley (ed.) New York, Grune & Stratton, 1971

———. "Observation of the Family of the Schizophrenic." *Amer. J. of Orthopsychiatry* 30 (1960): 460–467

———. *Strategies of Psychotherapy.* New York, Grune & Stratton, 1963

———. "The Art of Psychoanalysis," in *The Strategies of Psychotherapy.* New York, Grune & Stratton, 1963

———. "The Control of Fear with Hypnosis." *Amer. J. of Clinical Hypnosis* 2 (1960): 109–115

———. "The Power Tactics of Jesus Christ." In *The Power Tactics of Jesus Christ.* New York, Grossman Publ, 1969

———. "Toward a Theory of Pathological Systems." In *Family Therapy and Disturbed Families.* G. Zuk, I. Boszormenyi-Nagy (eds). Palo Alto, Science and Behavior Books, 1967

———. *Uncommon Therapy.* New York, W. W. Norton, 1973

———. "Whither Family Therapy?" In *The Power Tactics of Jesus Christ.* New York, Grossman Publ, 1969

Hall, A, and Fagen, D. "Definition of a System." *General System Yearbook* 1 (1956): 18–28

Heidegger, Martin. *"Being and Time."* New York, Harper & Row, 1966

Hoffman, Lynn. "Deviation-Amplifying Processes," In *Changing Families.* New York, Grune & Stratton, 1971

Howard, Jane. *Please Touch.* New York, McGraw-Hill, 1970

Howells, John. *Family Psychiatry.* Springfield, Charles C. Thomas, 1963

———. *Theory and Practice of Family Psychiatry.* New York, Brunner/Mazel, 1971

Jackson, Don. "Differences Between 'Normal' and 'Abnormal' Families." In *Expanding Theory and Practice in Family Therapy.* N. Ackerman, F. Beatman, S. Sherman. (eds). New York, Family Association of America, 1967

———. "Family Rules: Marital Quid Pro Quo." *Archives of General Psychiatry* 12 (1965): 589–594

———. "The Eternal Triangle." In *Techniques of Family Therapy.* J. Haley and L. Hoffman (eds). New York, Basic Books, 1967

———. "The Question of Family Homeostasis." In *Communication, Family, and Marriage.* D. Jackson (ed). Palo Alto, Science & Behavior Books, 1968

Jackson, Don and Haley, Jay. "Transference Revisited." In *Therapy, Communication, and Change.* Palo Alto, Science & Behavior Books, 1968

Jackson, Don and Satir, Virginia. "A Review of Psychiatric Developments in Family Diagnosis and Family Therapy." In *Exploring the Base for Family Therapy,* N. Ackerman, F. Beatman, S. Sherman (eds). New York, Family Association of America, 1961

Jackson, Don and Weakland, John. "Conjoint Family Therapy: Some Considerations on Theory, Technique and Results." *Psychiatry* 24 (1961): 30–45

———. "Schizophrenic Symptoms and Family Interaction." *Archives of Gen. Psychiatry* 1 (1959), 618–621

Jackson, Don, and Yalom, Irvin. "Conjoint Family Therapy as an Aid to Intensive Psychotherapy." In *Modern Psychotherapeutic Practice.* A. Burton (ed). Palo Alto, Science and Behavior Books, 1965

Klein, Melanie. *The Psychoanalysis of Children.* London, Hogarth Press, 1932

Laing, Ronald. *Knots.* New York, Pantheon Books, 1970

———. "Mystification, Confusion, and Conflict." In *Intensive Family Therapy.* I. Boszormenyi-Nagy, J. Framo (ed). New York, Harper and Row, 1965

———. *The Divided Self.* Pelican Edition. Baltimore, Penguin Books, 1965

———. *The Politics of Experience.* New York, Ballantine Books, 1967

———. *The Self and Others.* 2nd Revised Edition. New York, Pantheon Books, 1969

Laing, Ronald, and Cooper, D. *Reason and Violence: A Decade of Sartre's Philosophy— 1950–1960.* London, Tavistock Publications, 1964

Laing, Ronald, and Esterson, Aaron. *Sanity, Madness and the Family.* Baltimore, Penguin Books, 1964

Laqueur, H. Peter. "Multiple Family Therapy: Questions and Answers." In *Techniques of Family Therapy A Primer.*

D. Bloch (ed). New York, Grune & Stratton, 1973

Laqueur, H. Peter; Laburt, Harry; and Morong, Eugene. "Multiple Family Therapy: Further Developments." In *Changing Families*. J. Haley (ed). New York, Grune & Stratton, 1971

Lederer, William, and Jackson, Don. *The Mirages of Marriage*. New York, W. W. Norton, 1968

Levenson, Edgar. *The Fallacy of Understanding*. New York, Basic Books, 1972

Lidz, Theodore. "Family Organization and Personality Structure." In *A Modern Introduction to the Family*. N. Bell, E. Vogel (eds). Revised Edition. New York, Free Press, 1968

———. "Schizophrenia and the Family." *Psychiatry* 21 (1958): 21–27

Lidz, Theodore, and Fleck, Stephen. "Family Studies and a Theory of Schizophrenia." In *Schizophrenia and the Family*. T. Lidz, S. Fleck, A. Cornelison. (eds) New York, International University Press, 1965

———. "Schizophrenia, Human Integration and the Role of the Family." In the *Etiology of Schizophrenia*. D. Jackson (ed). New York, Basic Books, 1960

Lidz, Theodore, *et al.* "The Intrafamilial Environment of the Schizophrenic Patient: 6. The Transmission of Irrationality," *Arch Neurn Psychiatry* 79 (1958): 305–316

Lieberman, Morton; Yalom, Irvin;

Miles, Matthew. *Encounter Groups: First Facts.* New York, Basic Books, 1973

MacGregor, Robert, *et al. Multiple Impact Therapy With Families.* New York, McGraw-Hill, 1964

Malinowski, Bronislaw. *Sex and Repression in a Savage Society.* New York, Meridian Press, 1955

Mead, Margaret. *The Coming of Age in Samoa.* New York, Wm. Morrow & Co., 1961

Meissner, William. "Thinking About the Family-Psychiatric Aspects." *Family Process* 3 (1964): 1–40

Midelfort, Christian. *The Family in Psychotherapy.* New York, McGraw-Hill, 1957

Minuchin, Salvador. "Family Therapy: Theory or Technique?" In *Science and Psychoanalysis.* Vol. 14, J. Masserman (ed). New York, Grune & Stratton, 1969

———. "Structural Family Therapy." In *American Handbook of Psychiatry*, Vol. 2, c 11, G Caplan (ed). New York, Basic Books, 1974

Minuchin, Salvador, and Barcai, Avnar. "Therapeutically Induced Family Crisis." In *Science and Psychoanalysis.* Vol. 14. J. Masserman (ed). New York, Grune & Stratton, 1969

Minuchin, Salvador; Montalvo, Braulio; Guerney, Bernard Jr.; Rosman, Bernice; Schumer, Florence. *Families of the Slums.* New York, Basic Books, 1967

Mitchell, Celia. "Problems and Principles in Family Therapy." In *Expanding Theory and Practice in Family Therapy.* N. Ackerman, F. Beatman, S. Sherman (eds). New York, Family Service Association, 1967

Morris, G, and Wynne, Lyman. "Schizophrenic Offspring and Parental Styles of Communications: Predictive Study Using Family Therapy Excerpts." *Psychiatry* 28 (1965): 32–39

Olson, David. "Marital and Family Therapy: Integrative Review and Critique." *Journal of Marriage and the Family* 32 (1970): 501–538

Papp, Peggy; Silverstein, Olga; Carter, Elizabeth. "Family Sculpting in Preventive Work with "Well Families." *Family Process* 12: 197–212

Parsons, Talcott. "The Incest Taboo in Relation to Social Structure and the Socialization of the Child." *British Journal of Sociology* 5 (1954): 101–117

Parsons, Talcott and Bales, Robert. *Family, Socialization and Interaction Process.* New York, The Free Press, 1955

Pavenstedt, Eleanor. "A Comparison of the Child-Rearing Environment of Upper-Lower and Very Low-Lower Class Families." *American Journal of Orthopsychiatry* 35: 89–95

Rogers, Carl. *Client-Centered Therapy.* Boston, Houghton Mifflin Co., 1951

Ruesch, Jurgen and Bateson, Gregory. *Communication: The Social Matrix of Psychiatry.* New York, W. W. Norton, 1951

Ryckoff, Irving; Day, Juliana; and Wynne, Lyman. "Maintenance of Stereotyped Roles in Families of Schizophrenics. *Archives of General Psychiatry* I (1959): 93–98

Sager, Clifford; Brayboy, Thomas; Waxonberg, Barbara. *Black Ghetto Family in Therapy: A Laboratory Experience.* New York, Grove Press, 1970

Satir, Virginia. "A Family of Angels." In *Techniques of Family Therapy.* J. Haley, L. Hoffman (eds). New York, Basic Books, 1967

———. *Conjoint Family Therapy.* 2nd Revised Edition. Palo Alto, Science and Behavior Books, 1967

———. *Peoplemaking.* Palo Alto, Science & Behavior Books, 1972

———. "The Family as a Treatment Unit." In *Changing Families.* J. Haley (ed). New York, Grune & Stratton, 1971

Schaffer, L; Wynne, Lyman; Day, Juliana; Ryckoff, Irving; and Halperin, A. "On the Nature and Sources of the Psychiatric Experience with the Family of the Schizophrenia." *Psychiatry* 25 (1962): 32–45

Searles, Harold. "The Effort to Drive the Other Person Crazy —An Element in the Aetiology and Psychotherapy of Schizophrenia." British Journal of Medical Psychology 32 (1959): 1–18

Singer, Margaret and Wynne, Lyman. "Thought Disorder and Family Relations of Schizophrenics, II; Classification of Forms of Thinking." *Arch. of Gen. Psychiatry* 9 (1963): 199–206

———. "Thought Disorder and Family Relations of Schizophrenics, III: Methodology Using Projective Techniques." *Arch. of Gen. Psychiatry* 121 (1965): 186–200

———. "Thought Disorder and Family Relations of Schizophrenics, IV. Results and Implications." *Arch. of Gen. Psychiatry* 12 (1965): 201–212

Speck, Ross, and Attneave, Carolyn. *Family Networks*. New York, Pantheon Books, 1973

Spiegel, John. "Some Cultural Aspects of Transference and Counter-transference." In *Science and Psychoanalysis*, Vol II. J. Masserman (ed). New York, Grune & Stratton, 1956

———. "The Resolution of Role Conflict Within the Family." *Psychiatry* 20 (1957): 1–16

———. *Transactions—The Interplay Between Individual, Family and Society*. New York, Science House, 1971

Sullivan, Harry Stack. *The Interpersonal Theory of Psychiatry*. New York, W. W. Norton, 1953

Toman, Walter, *Family Constellation*. New York, Springer Publishing Co., 1961

von Bertalanffy, Ludwig. "General System Theory and Psychiatry." In *American Handbook of Psychiatry*. Vol 3. S. Arieti (ed). New York, Basic Books, 1966

———. "The Meaning of General System Theory." In *General System Theory*. New York, George Braziller, 1968

Watzlawick, Paul; Beavin, Janet; and Jackson, Don. *Pragmatics of Human Communication*. New York, W. W. Norton, 1967

Watzlawick, Paul. "A Review of the Double Bind Theory—1962." In *Communication, Family and Marriage*. D. Jackson (ed). Palo Alto, Science and Behavior Books, 1968

Whitehead, Alfred, and Russell, Bertrand. *"Principia Mathematica*. Second Edition. New York, W. W. Norton, 1938

Williams, Tennessee. *The Glass Menagerie*. New York, New Directions, 1966

Wynne, Lyman. "Family Relations of A Set of Monozygotic Quadruplet Schizophrenics." *Orell Fuscli Graphiques* 2 (1957): 43–49

———. "Some Guidelines for Exploratory Conjoint Family Therapy." In *Changing Families*. J. Haley (ed). New York, Grune & Stratton, 1971

———. "Some Indications and Contraindications for Exploratory Family Therapy." In *Intensive Family Therapy*. I. Boszormenyi-Nagy, J. Framo (eds). New York, Harper & Row. 1965

———. "The Study of Intrafamilial Alignments and Splits in Exploratory Family Therapy."

In *Exploring the Base for Family Therapy.* N. Ackerman, F. Beatman, S. Sherman (eds). New York, Family Service Association, 1961

Wynne, Lyman; Ryckoff, Irving; Day, Juliana; and Hirsch, Stanley. "Pseudomutuality in the Family Relations of Schizophrenics," *Psychiatry* 21 (1958): 205–220

Wynne, Lyman and Singer, Margaret. "Thought Disorder and Family Relations of Schizophrenics, I: Research Strategy." *Arch of Gen. Psychiatry* 9 (1963): 191–198

Yalom, Irvin. *The Theory and Practice of Group Psychotherapy.* New York, Basic Books, 1970

Zuk, Gerald. *Family Therapy: A Triadic-Based Approach.* New York, Behavioral Publications, 1971

Author Index

SUBJECT INDEX